# How To Get
# *All*
# Your
# Family Saved

*by Philip Cameron*

Philip Cameron Ministries
P.O. Box 241241
Montgomery, AL 36124

# Dedication

I dedicate this book to my wife, Chrissie, who has always encouraged me to follow His voice, whether it led us close to home or across the sea. With your quiet strength, you have always been to me like the virtuous woman of Proverbs 31:10, "worth more than precious gems." And...

To my son, Philip. Now you stand at the threshold of adulthood and I honestly can't believe it. To see you yearn for God and watch you obey His voice makes your dad more proud than you will ever know.

To Melody, my song. If all the world could see me as you do, I would be king of the earth. I can't believe you came from me... I hold you and Heaven smiles.

To Andrew, my chosen one. Heaven moved me around the world to find you. The moment I saw you standing in your crib at the orphanage, God let me know you were mine. Your gentleness and caring come from God. Andy, you are tangible proof of a merciful God. Daddy loves you!

To Lauren Ann, my blessed surprise! Your coming was a surprise and in every way you have made every day of my life a fresh new experience. Of all our kids, you... make me pray for me. Then I do what all dads who love God do... I give you all to His care.

# Acknowledgment

I would like to thank my friend of over twenty years, Brian Paterson, for his invaluable help in putting this book together. His labors make it possible for me to get ideas and thoughts out of my head and on to paper, and I simply couldn't have completed a project like this without the benefit of his scholarly precision and perceptive counsel.

—Philip Cameron

# Contents

# Introduction

Does God want to save your family? That might sound like a strange question, but, sadly, many Christians seem to have concluded that God isn't too interested one way or the other. That's a curious way for people to think who profess to follow the love-driven teachings of the Gospel. If such a conclusion were true, either God doesn't love our family members as much as He loves us, or else, having saved us, He somehow doesn't mind letting the rest of our loved ones be lost for all eternity.

Both of those last two propositions being just too nonsensical to accept, let's consider a couple of more likely possibilities: 1) We're having trouble accepting the daunting responsibility of being God's representative (possibly the only one) in the "mission field" that consists of our unsaved loved ones; or 2) We haven't discovered or taken advantage of the Scriptural and spiritual "ammunition" God has made available to us. We need that ammunition because we are in a battle with an enemy who is hungry for the souls of our family members. Thankfully, this is a battle we can certainly win and one we don't need to fight alone!

In this volume, we'll make the case from Scripture that God most certainly is interested in saving your family. In fact, from the inception of God's dealings with humanity, He has been consumed with the value and importance of the family. He instituted the family; the Scriptures reveal a divine thought process that revolves around the family; and as He unfolded the plan of salvation through the sacrifice of His own Son, that plan was unmistakably designed to gather entire families into the Gospel net.

This book has one goal: to help Christians win their unsaved loved ones to Christ. There are lots of other fine instructional Christian books and publications that deal in depth with family-related subjects like parenting, marriage and so forth. I've been helped and blessed by several I could recommend to you, but I must make clear at the outset that this is not one of those kinds of books. We'll certainly look at aspects of parenting, spousal relationships and other relationships within the family, but all from a foundation of helping you become the catalyst that sparks an outpouring of repentance and salvation among your loved ones.

I've also tried to avoid any suggestion that there is some simple "magic formula" to be utilized. Winning your loved ones to Christ takes dedication, persistence and wisdom. It's hard work! However, we do have help—major help! Only the Holy Spirit can convict a man or woman of sin, but that same Holy Spirit can use you, your lifestyle, your speech, your compassion, your example, to bring your loved one face to face with undeniable truth, precipitating the opportunities needed for His convicting power to do its life-changing work.

Obviously, God will not override the free will He has graciously given to every one of us. I completely agree with those who say that God will not force Himself into the heart of someone who wishes to reject Him. But that's no excuse for not praying, or not witnessing through our lives as well as our words, or for giving up on anyone, especially someone in our own family. There are lots of stubborn people in the world, but God isn't willing that anyone should perish, not even the stubborn ones. Stubborn or not, your unsaved family members are loved of God, and His plan and desire is to save their eternal souls. His plan also calls for you, whom He has redeemed and called by your name, to be the carrier of His Word, the messenger of life to your loved ones. My prayer is that this book will help you do just that.

# Chapter One

# Hebrews 11– The Household Salvation Chapter

In the great faith chapter, Hebrews 11, the writer presents the famous roll-call of the heroes of Scripture that has become known as the "Hall of Faith." Naturally, this is a tremendous chapter for use in the study of the subject of faith. I rejoice in the great revelations given to those chosen by God to help break the Church out of the "poverty cycle" that has plagued so many people over the years, but there's a trap we Christians can fall prey to here. It's a semantic trap initially, but the fallout can affect a whole lot more than our words. The word faith has become almost synonymous with terms like prosperity or healing or other aspects of what is called "victorious living." Let me be clear—I do believe God wants to bless you, and He also wants you to prosper and be in health (3 Jn. v.2). My spirit has been uplifted so many times by many of the anointed men and women God has called to teach on the subject of faith, however, faith isn't just about prosperity or health. I appreciate teaching that says

God wants you to be blessed in those areas, but I object when that teaching is so focused on them that its vision of a life of faith seems to involve little more than attaining personal comfort and convenience.

We must never reduce God to the role of some kind of celestial errand boy. It's my job to serve Him, not the other way round. Yes, He is a good God who cares for us and who has promised to meet our needs. Yes, He is still a God of miracles, whose provision for His children is nothing less than astounding—I'll be the first one to testify to that! But let's not forget we have a job to do. There's only one thing you and I can do that generates so much excitement in Heaven the very angels of God start to rejoice, and that's when we help just one person come to Christ (Lu. 15:10). If you ask me, the real purpose of living by faith is to keep those angels singing! And if they happen to be singing about someone in your family coming to Christ, I tend to think there will be more than a little celebration going on in your neck of the woods as well.

### What Makes a Hero?

People are inducted into a "Hall of Fame" because of their unique achievements or talents. They are a cut above the average, and it is generally deemed a great honor for a sports personality, for example, to be inducted into the Hall of Fame for his particular sport. In the same way, we can look at the

"Hall of Faith" in Hebrews 11 and see that those included are there solely because they distinguished themselves among their contemporaries and became heroes of faith. As you go through the characters referred to in this chapter, you'll find a "who's who" of Scripture. From Abel to Noah then on to Samuel, these are some of history's most significant and influential people. They were all written into the divine record and included in this "Hall of Faith" because God wanted us to learn what faith is and what it is in the heart of a man or woman that can bring great faith to bear on one's circumstances.

Verses 33 and 34 tell us some of the accomplishments of these heroes of faith:

"Who through faith subdued kingdoms, wrought righteousness, obtained promises, stopped the mouths of lions.

"Quenched the violence of fire, escaped the edge of the sword, out of weakness were made strong, waxed valiant in fight, turned to flight the armies of the aliens."

Well, doesn't that sound like it's exactly what all those proponents of "victorious living" are talking about? It does, but, as always, there's more. Verses 35 to 38 go on to say that the heroes of faith were also called upon in some other ways:

"Women received their dead raised to life again: and others were tortured, not accepting deliverance; that they might obtain a better resurrection:

"And others had trial of cruel mockings and scourgings, yea, moreover of bonds and imprisonment:

"They were stoned, they were sawn asunder, were tempted, were slain with the sword: they wandered about in sheepskins and goatskins; being destitute, afflicted, tormented;

"(Of whom the world was not worthy:) they wandered in deserts, and in mountains, and in dens and caves of the earth."

Doesn't sound to me like those folks encountered an over-abundance of personal comfort and convenience. Don't forget, these people were Scripture's greatest examples of living by faith, yet they were "destitute, afflicted, tormented." I'm afraid many people have suffered a glaring educational gap in the area of faith, sort of like trying to pursue a degree in English Literature without ever studying Shakespeare.

## *Faith—for the Family*

"Wait a minute," I can hear you saying. "What's all this got to do with Household Salvation?" My contention is that Hebrews 11 isn't about what you might think it's about. When you dig into the lives of these men and women of faith, you'll discover that what actually drove them was their obedience to God and their desire to appropriate His promises not only to them, but to their seed—*to their families!*

14

Hebrews 11 takes us from the time of Adam and his children to the period of Samuel and the installation of the monarchy in Israel, at about 1053 B.C. That's almost a three thousand year chunk of Old Testament history, so, if we want to provide a Scriptural basis for our thoughts on Household Salvation, Hebrews 11 makes a very good place to start.

I like the Living Bible's rendition of the first two verses:

"What is faith? It is the confident assurance that something we want is going to happen. It is the certainty that what we hope for is waiting for us, even though we cannot see it up ahead.

"Men of God in days of old were famous for their faith." (He. 11:1,2 TLB)

I can think of a lot of famous people in today's society, but not too many who are idolized or touted in the mainstream media have become famous for their faith. In Christian circles we can certainly think of some outstanding individuals whom we might call famous, at least as far as the Church is concerned, but in the world as a whole, most are famous for very different reasons. What a testimony it would be to have people look back on our lives and say something like, "What a life of faith they lived!"

The problem is, if you'll look at verse 1 again, faith is something we must hold onto with "the certainty that what we hope for is waiting for us, *even though we cannot see it up ahead.*" To operate in faith is to keep believing despite the present circumstances, despite opposition, persecution, discouragement and even our own impatience. This concept couldn't be more relevant to the subject of Household Salvation. It can be an enormous challenge to keep believing when it *appears* that one's unsaved family members are further from coming to Christ than they ever were. When you begin to pray for and work towards the salvation of a loved one, the circumstances surrounding that person can sometimes appear to be getting worse than they were to start with. It's comforting to realize that it may be Satan making a last-ditch effort to keep them from getting saved, but until victory is actually achieved in that loved one's life, it can get very hard on the person doing the praying. Discouragement can come from many sources, be it a well-meaning friend who tells you that your prayers are "wasted on that rascal" or it could be that you simply become "weary in well-doing." Faith is what withstands these difficulties, and that's one lesson we can definitely learn from the heroes of faith in Hebrews 11.

Verse 6 reinforces the point: "But without faith it is impossible to please him: for he that cometh to God must believe that he is, and that he is a rewarder of them that diligently seek him." He is a rewarder of them who seek Him *diligently!* Winning your family to Christ is a reward worth the dedication it demands in your life. It means setting a standard in your own lifestyle that serves as a beacon to those in your family still living in spiritual darkness. While it doesn't mean developing a "holier than thou" attitude, seeming to think of yourself as "better" than others—after all, we've all sinned and come short of the glory of God—it does mean showing your loved ones that you're prepared to "walk the walk" not just "talk the talk."

## *Called By Your Name!*

Throughout Scripture, God made it very clear to Israel what kind of relationship He wanted to have with them as a nation, as individuals and as families. Isaiah 43:1 says this:

"But now thus saith the LORD that created thee, O Jacob, and he that formed thee, O Israel, Fear not: for I have redeemed thee, I have called thee by thy name; thou art mine."

The phrase "called thee by thy name" has more significance than some might realize. We know God claimed Israel as His own on the basis of four factors: (1) creation, (2) formation, (3) redemption, and (4) naming, which according to ancient custom signified ownership. I've spent a great deal of time in Eastern Europe, particularly in Romania. In many such countries, there are traditions still in use that emphasize the importance, not of the first name, but of the last name, the *family* name. When someone writes their name down, even on a non-formal document, they don't do as we would and write "John Smith," or whatever their name is, they'll write, "Smith John." When they answer the telephone, they'll announce, "Family Smith!"

Even in Western society, it is the last name that links us to our background and position in life, that tells others who we are in relation to the rest of society. The last name carries history with it and is our link with past generations. Back in the old days in my native Scotland, people were identified according to a very carefully organized clan system. I can look back over centuries of history related to the name Cameron and see exactly where I came from. Back then, if you didn't belong to one of the major clans, you could form an alliance with one, which afforded you the protection of the clan and gave you the right to wear the clan colors, the tartan patterns which were unique to each clan. The patterns on the kilts and other tartan items worn by those you'll see wearing traditional Scottish garb are specific to each family and, even today, it is not considered "good form" to wear a tartan pattern which your family name does not entitle you to wear. If I had been alive a few hundred years ago, I would have been very careful to wear the tartan of the large and powerful Cameron clan. Any potential enemies would know that to pick a fight with me was not something my numerous kinsmen would take kindly to.

Back in those days, it would have been normal to say, "I am of the House of Cameron," referring of course not to the building one lived in, but to one's family connections. So when I read, "Believe on the Lord Jesus Christ, and thou shalt be saved, *AND THY HOUSE*," (Ac. 16:31), my background automatically gives me a whole lot to think about where my family is concerned. I can imagine God saying, "I have redeemed thee, I have called thee by thy name—Cameron!" Put your own last name in there, and realize that we serve a God who has always shown Himself to think in terms of the family:

"For as the new heavens and the new earth Which I will make shall remain before Me," says the LORD, "So shall your descendants and your name remain." (Is. 66:22, NKJV).

In Scripture, rarely is an individual mentioned without reference to his family and his tribe. God, while certainly interested in the individual, is making sure we understand that His love is extended to entire families. He knows *you*, He has called you by your (family) name, and He has made provision in His plan of redemption for you... *and your house!* "For Jacob my servant's sake, and Israel mine elect, I have even called thee by thy name: I have *surnamed* thee, though thou hast not known me." (Is. 45:4).

### *Heroes of Faith—Heroes of Household Salvation*

Let's go to Hebrews 11:7 and start taking a closer look at the Household Salvation connection in the lives of these heroes of faith:

"By faith Noah, being warned of God of things not seen as yet, moved with fear, prepared an ark *to the saving of his house;* by the which he condemned the world, and became heir of the righteousness which is by faith."

Noah's motivation for building the ark wasn't just to keep some animals dry. An animal lover he may have been, but there was a whole lot more going on than that. Firstly, He was being obedient to God. God told him to do it and that was all the reason this righteous man needed. He must have known the task wasn't going to be easy, and indeed it wasn't. He endured ridicule and hardship that didn't just last for a week or two or even for a year or two. He had to push his way through enormous obstacles and remain faithful to God for *a hundred and twenty years!* Why would someone do all that? According to verse 7, he prepared the ark *"to the saving of his house"* He built that ark because he wanted to save his family from the judgement God was about to send on the world!

Noah knew how sad and angry God was at the depths of evil to which mankind had sunk (Gen. 6:5,6). God declared that this state of affairs would not be allowed to continue: "I will give him (the human race) 120 years to mend his ways." (Gen. 6:3 TLB). Since Noah entered the Ark when he was 600 years old (Gen. 7:6), he must have been 480 years old when God told him to start building. The interesting thing about that is, his first son, Shem, wasn't born till Noah was 500 years old (Gen. 5:32). That means Noah must have started building the ark to save his family *20 years before he even had any children!*

## Build Your Ark!

In your situation, as you believe God and dedicate yourself to winning your loved ones to Jesus, what you are doing is building an ark to the saving of your household. Jesus said, "As it was in the days of Noah, so it will be at the coming of the Son of Man." (Mt. 24:37 NIV). If we believe we are in the "last days" before Jesus returns, what we are saying is, these are the "days of Noah." When Noah was faced with God's impending judgement on humanity, he was obedient and built the ark to ensure his family's safety. As the human race approaches judgement once more, I have to ask, how well are you building your ark? This isn't something to be done in a careless way. Lives are at stake. The fate of eternal souls rests on how well you build this ark. If Noah hadn't followed God's very explicit directions as to how the ark was to be built, who's to say that the vessel wouldn't have been smashed to pieces when the first heavy wave hit it? I'm sure there must have been days when Noah would have preferred to be doing something else, or maybe he didn't want to use a certain thickness or type of wood, or perhaps he felt it would have been easier on him if he didn't have to use quite as much of that horrible, foul-smelling pitch all over the place. But, whatever he felt like, he didn't take any shortcuts, he did precisely what God told him to do.

God's instructions to you and I concerning our families are no less explicit. We can't be effective witnesses if we're living disobedient lives; we can't expect our families to become convinced of the love of Christ if we never demonstrate it; and we can't build a useful ark for our loved ones if we don't pay attention to the details. To put it another way, when it comes to the ark *you* are building for the saving of *your* house, are all your planks in place?

I'm simply saying that God wants you and I to create a place of safety where our unsaved loved ones can find escape from the storms of sin raging in our world today. When they're in your house, they'll find you there cultivating a relationship with God. They'll see His love in the way you live, speak and act, and, when the time is right, they'll hear God's own Word come out of your mouth telling them how to come to Him. They'll have no doubt whatsoever that the words they hear are matched by the life you've led... if you're building the ark right!

Your loved ones may not always appreciate what you're trying to do; they may even actively resent it. But when the floods of life—and we've all faced them—start washing away their hopes, their dreams, and all the ideas they had that once sounded so grand and so important, that's when they need to know you've built an ark.

In later chapters we'll look at some of the practical things you can do to make sure your family's ark is in good shape, but for now, start by asking God to give you a "Noah anointing!" That's an anointing to keep building your ark no matter what the personal cost, how bad the public ridicule, or the how large the obstacles in your path.

Noah is included in the "Hall of Faith" because he took God at His word, then he did something about it—he built an ark *to the saving of his house!*

# Chapter Two

# Heroes of Faith– The Household Salvation Connection

We're going to continue our look at the Household Salvation connection in the lives of the great heroes of faith from Hebrews 11. After Noah, the next person mentioned is instantly recognizable as one of the most significant of all Old Testament figures. Abraham certainly fits the bill as one of those who was "famous for his faith." Verses 8 and 9 have this to say about him:

"By faith Abraham, when he was called to go out into a place which he should after receive for an inheritance, obeyed; and he went out, not knowing whither he went.

"By faith he sojourned in the land of promise, as in a strange country, *dwelling in tabernacles with Isaac and Jacob, the heirs with him of the same promise:*

"For he looked for a city which hath foundations, whose builder and maker is God."

Abraham was as blessed and prosperous in Ur of the Chaldees as anyone would have wanted to be. He wasn't driven out by enemies, nor had he suffered financial ruin or any other personal disaster. He had no reason to leave home and wander in a strange land except that he wanted to obey God and receive His promises. God declared that Abraham would be the progenitor of a great nation (Gen. 12:1-3). God also promised Abraham that he would give the land of Canaan to *his seed.* That of course meant God expected Abraham and Sarah to become parents, which had to have been hard for them to believe when you consider that Abraham was already 75 years old when he left Ur (Gen 12:4), and his wife, Sarah, was 65, and they were still childless.

It took 25 years of sojourn in the land of Canaan before his son, Isaac was born, and Abraham had plenty of opposition to deal with along the way. The Bible says that even when Abraham first arrived in Canaan, he had to contend with the land's inhabitants, yet, despite the dangers, one of the first things he did was to build an altar to Jehovah (Gen 12:6,7).

Let's not forget Sarah, who is also given a place of honor in the "Hall of Faith" in her own right:

"Through faith also Sara herself received strength to conceive seed, and was delivered of a child when she was past age, because she judged him faithful who had promised. (Verse 11).

She was ninety years old when she gave birth to h first child. For twenty five years she and

Abraham held on to an impossible dream—but with God, nothing is impossible! As unlikely as it may appear that your unsaved loved one will turn away from a life of sin and give his or her life to Christ, it is no more unlikely than an old woman like Sarah giving birth.

## *Blessing the Families of the Earth*

Abraham and Sarah bearing a son was indeed a miracle, but something far more significant was also accomplished. From them there came "so many as the stars of the sky in multitude, and as the sand which is by the sea shore innumerable." (Verse 12). God spoke repeatedly concerning Abraham's seed, and that his seed would be used to bless the world: "And I will bless them that bless thee, and curse him that curseth thee: and in thee shall all *families* of the earth be blessed." (Gen. 12:3).

That "Seed" who would bless the world (and the families of the world) is Christ himself: "Now to Abraham and his seed were the promises made. He saith not, And to seeds, as of many; but as of one, And to thy seed, which is Christ." (Gal. 3:16). God didn't just say that through Abraham all individuals would be blessed, but all *families* of the earth would be blessed. God loves families, He moves in families, and His heart longs to touch and bless not only you, but your entire family!

## *Don't Do God's Job*

Everything Abraham did seemed to revolve around his passion for the future of his family. Even when his faith faltered and he had a child by Sarah's maidservant, Hagar (Gen. 16:1-4), it was his attempt to humanly manipulate the fulfillment of God's promise of a seed. It was clearly a mistake and neither he nor Sarah would have made it into the "Hall of Faith" based on their actions that day. Thankfully, you and I can learn something from the mistakes of the heroes of faith, not just from the things they did right. What followed Abraham and Sarah's impatience and lack of trust in God can be summed up in one word: trouble! In practical terms, there are certain things you and I could and should do as we labor to win our loved ones to Christ, and we're going to look at those things in detail later, but there are some things we can't do anything about and we need to learn to leave them to God!

In the birth process, assuming all is progressing normally, a baby won't be born until it's good and ready. Modern medicine can help things along but until all the correct chemical and physiological changes have taken place and all the right signals are sent to all the right places, that baby isn't going anywhere. Sometimes, in my opinion, when it comes to our families' salvation, we can get in the way of the birth process, the "new birth" process that is. We try to convict them of sin, when only the Holy Spirit can do that. Because of our overwhelming desire to see our family members living for Christ, we might get impatient with an unsaved loved one who is acting, well, like an unsaved loved one. We forget they're not acting like saved people because that's not who they are. So we fly off the handle over whatever it is they've done and end up possibly missing an opportunity to accomplish something in their lives that love, patience and wisdom might have brought about. I'm in no way suggesting that as Christians we can condone sin, and we certainly can't stand idly by if the actions of that loved one are causing actual pain or suffering—but let's choose our confrontations wisely! There are some things about an unsaved loved one's lifestyle that may annoy us, but if they're only annoying and not imminently harmful, perhaps we just need to commit those things to the Lord for a while longer. Frustration and impatience might lead to withering criticism over some issue which in and of itself may not be all that significant. However, there's no telling how long the fallout from those hastily spoken words might affect your ability to advance the cause of winning your loved one to Christ.

Getting back to the birth process, the flip side of that coin is, when the baby's ready to come, there's no stopping it! And when the Holy Spirit has done his convicting work in the life of your loved one, when the forces of Hell can no longer withstand your prayers and your Godly influence, that loved one is going to leave behind all those "annoying" but now trivial things, and rejoice with you as a new member of the household of faith!

Abraham got in the way of what God was doing and triggered unprecedented strife in his household. Yet God honored his promises to Abraham, and his son Isaac was born when Abraham was *one hundred years old!* Your promise may be a long time coming, but don't give up, don't get impatient, and embrace the promises of God to you and your household with all your heart!

## *Isaac*

The next member of the "Hall of Faith" mentioned in Hebrews 11 is Abraham's "child of promise," Isaac. There's something a bit different about Isaac as opposed to most of the other people mentioned here. Most of our heroes of faith had times when they really showed their mettle. Although they all had times of failure and despair, there were also those special moments when the men were "macho" and heroic and the women were brave and stalwart. It's hard to find any incidents like those in the life of Isaac. He certainly wasn't a bad man, it's just that at times he seemed to be a bit slow on the uptake. In today's vernacular, some might say he wasn't playing with a full deck. He was blessed for all that, being the heir to the wealth of Abraham, but he definitely had some intellectual lapses. He didn't believe his own ears when he was tricked into passing on the blessing to Jacob instead of Esau.

"You sound like Jacob, but you feel like Esau, therefore you are Esau." That's not an exact quote, but it does show the peculiar kind of logic Isaac was capable of. Abraham didn't trust Isaac to pick his own wife, so he had it done for him. Later, when Isaac tried to trick Abimelech the king of the Philistines into thinking that Rebekah was his sister and not his wife, he then proceeded to act intimately with her in a public place. At times, the man just wasn't too bright.

### An "Uneventful" Life

There's an interesting quote about Isaac in *Halley's Bible Handbook*: "Not much is told of Isaac's life... (he) was prosperous and rich; peaceable; and his life uneventful." In other words, apart from the fact that he was Abraham's son, he was a pretty average Joe. He had his good days and his bad days, never achieved anything we might call outstanding, but lived a fairly comfortable, satisfying life. Yet, there's something important to realize about this "average" man. When God sent Moses to free the children of Israel, He told him to use a certain identifying phrase to establish his credentials as one sent from God:

"And God said moreover unto Moses, Thus shalt thou say unto the children of Israel, The LORD God of your fathers, *the God of Abraham, the God of Isaac, and the God of Jacob*, hath sent me unto you:

this is my name for ever, and this is my memorial unto all generations." (Ex. 3:15).

God obviously felt there was something worthy in Isaac if He wanted to be known "unto all generations" as Isaac's God. We can all understand why God is the God of Abraham. From just the brief look taken earlier in this chapter, it's not hard to tell that he was a great, faith-filled individual. As far as Jacob is concerned, his life reads like an adventure novel. He was the rascal who, despite his faults, held on to the blessing of God for all he was worth. Jacob alone was the direct progenitor of the tribes of Israel; in fact it is Jacob who is first called Israel, the "friend of God." The point is, it's wonderful to know that God is the God of the great and faithful like Abraham. It's also a comfort that He is the God of a scoundrel like Jacob, that He can use such people despite the flaws in their character. I don't know about you, though, but sometimes I feel a bit like Isaac. Just bumbling along, making mistakes and trying to make the best of things. Isaac is "one of us," an average guy who nevertheless loved God. The wonderful thing is, God isn't just Abraham's God, and He isn't just Jacob's God, He is Isaac's God. Be encouraged! You don't have to be a genius for God to use you. You don't need great talent, or a dynamic personality, nor must you be one of those with an incredible testimony about being delivered from some terrible lifestyle. Thank God for those folks, but, for the regular, everyday folks who make up most of Church—rejoice! He is *your* God, and He intends to use you too!

## *One Great Achievement*

As we look for the Household Salvation connection in Isaac's life, there's just one achievement of his mentioned in the "Hall of Faith":

"By faith Isaac blessed Jacob and Esau concerning things to come." (He. 11:20).

Despite whatever failings he may have had, Isaac did one thing absolutely right, and that had to do with what he passed on to the next generation. He received blessing and an incredible inheritance from Abraham, and Abraham had also made him thoroughly familiar with God's promises. Isaac's great accomplishment, and it is the greatest accomplishment any of us can attain, was to pass on this Godly heritage to his children.

Again, what you need to get your family saved isn't great intellect or talent or any of the other things by which the world generally measures success. God can use those things and I don't mean to make light of such qualities, but what you really need if you're going to get your family saved is faith in the promises of God and a determined readiness to pass on your "inheritance" to the rest of your family. Isaac's life may have been somewhat uneventful by comparison to his peers in the "Hall of Faith," but what he did makes it possible for you and I to rejoice in the knowledge that "Abraham's blessings" remain in force today, that his Seed is continuing to bless the families of the earth, and that our families today can benefit from Isaac's carefully guarded legacy. As far as I'm concerned, Isaac more than deserves his place of honor in the "Hall of Faith!"

## *Jacob*

Jacob did something extraordinary, something very out of character for a man in the times in which he lived. He took the portion generally reserved for the firstborn (in this case, Reuben), by right of a process called primogeniture, and gave that portion to the sons of Joseph, Ephraim and Manasseh. Of course, Jacob knew first-hand what it was like to receive the blessing supposedly destined for an elder brother, but there was no trickery involved in his blessing of Joseph's sons:

"And (God) said unto me, Behold, I will make thee fruitful, and multiply thee, and I will make of thee a multitude of people; and will give this land to thy seed after thee for an everlasting possession. And now thy two sons, Ephraim and Manasseh, which were born unto thee in the land of Egypt before I came unto thee into Egypt, are mine; as Reuben and Simeon, they shall be mine." (Gen. 48:4,5).

Jacob's life was full of adventure and drama, and his relationship with God eventually reached such a place that he was able to say, "I have seen God face to face," (Gen. 32:30). This was no figurative statement, he really did come face to face with God.

34

Jacob wrestled with God, and learned that he had to depend upon Him, not on his own wily resourcefulness. Yet, given all those events for which he could have been remembered, his accolade in the "Hall of Faith" is simply this:

"By faith Jacob, when he was a dying, blessed both the sons of Joseph; and worshipped, leaning upon the top of his staff." (He. 11:21).

Of the 358 times you'll find Jacob's name mentioned in the King James Version of the Bible, this is the very last. It is his epitaph, and although written in language so innocuous it almost seems anti-climactic, it is, in fact, a record of his most significant act of faith. He saw beyond the evidence of his ageing eyes and beheld a day when his own sons, standing there before him, would father an entire nation. He saw the day when Joseph's children would yield not one but two of Israel's honored tribes, vital contributors to the development of the new nation. Their offspring would not remain in Egypt, but would at long-last become proud possessors of the land, heirs to the promise given by God to Abraham, passed on to Isaac, and then to Jacob himself.

Up until Jacob, God set aside individuals from the lineage that would become the nation of Israel. Jacob's brother Esau had been set aside, as had their father's brother, Ishmael. But there was to be no more setting aside, and Jacob was looking at the very men who would give birth to the tribes of Israel, the nation through whom God would send the Savior of all mankind.

At the same time, at the unction of God, he indicated the special reward, the "double-portion" inheritance, due to Joseph as the one God used to rescue this nation before it was even born. Jacob was doing more than just playing favorites, he was laying the groundwork for God's specific plan for His chosen people.

Nothing mattered more to Jacob at the time of his death than that his children obeyed God and became full beneficiaries of all His promises. He knew he wouldn't live to see the promise fulfilled with his natural eyes, but he saw it with the eyes of faith and he died wholeheartedly urging his children and his grandchildren to receive it. This point has perhaps already been made, but it bears repeating: When you see your family in their present state, with perhaps several members yet to receive Christ as their personal Savior, don't ever accept that as the final picture. Look ahead by faith, stand firmly upon the promises of God to you and your family, and work, pray and direct maximum effort towards the day when your entire family stands united in redemption.

## A Grandparent's Advantage

I can't conclude our look at Jacob without noting the special encouragement his story offers to grandparents. Modern traditions are obviously very different to those of Jacob's time, but grandparents are still in a unique position within the family structure. As Jacob did with Ephraim and Manasseh, grandparents can reach into the lives of their grandchildren in a way that no one else can. A saved grandparent can especially make an impact when there are smaller kids whose parents are not yet saved. I'm not talking about anything devious or that might cause concern to the parents, but a vigilant grandma or grandad will always be able to access prayer and storytelling (witnessing) opportunities that just won't come to anyone else. If your grown-up children are slow to pass on a Godly heritage to their kids, you may be the only one who can do something about it, and, like Jacob, you have the opportunity to leave a blessing with your grandchildren that will impact generations to come!

# Chapter Three

## More Household Salvation Heroes

It would obviously be possible to write in much greater detail about the heroes of faith we've looked at thus far, and, for this author at least, this is even more true concerning our next hero, Joseph. I love his story, but, since this is a book about Household Salvation and not just about any particular individual, let's get straight to the act for which Joseph is remembered in the "Hall of Faith":

"By faith Joseph, when he died, made mention of the departing of the children of Israel; and gave commandment concerning his bones." (He. 11:22).

Joseph was dying. This was no time to give attention to anything but the most significant, important things weighing on this Godly old man's heart. His final act, perhaps a little curious at first thought, was to extract an oath from the Children of Israel that they would bring his remains to the Promised Land when they departed from Egypt:

"And Joseph took an oath of the children of Israel, saying, God will surely visit you, and ye shall carry up my bones from hence." (Gen. 50:25).

Even though Joseph knew he wouldn't be physically alive to see the fulfillment of God's promise, he was still determined to participate in the inheritance God would give his descendants. The fact is, there would have been no inheritance for Israel had it not been for Joseph. If he had been so inclined, Joseph could have taken revenge on his brothers when they came to Egypt, and the rest of the family would have perished from the famine. But, despite all the hardships he endured at the hands of his brothers, his love for his family prevailed, and God used him to redeem not only those brothers, but their children, thereby preserving God's plan for the Children of Israel.

## *Overcoming Bitterness*

A little unforgiveness in Joseph's heart could have dramatically affected the course of human history. That same spirit of unforgiveness in our own hearts could just as dramatically affect the course of events for our families. If God is prepared to forgive that presently-unsaved family member and you aren't, you are putting your family's eternal destiny at risk! Nobody was more abused by his loved ones than Joseph. They threw him down a pit, sold him into slavery and then pretended to his father that he was dead. Thanks to them he ended up in prison. Few of us have experienced the rejection and lonely suffering that were heaped upon Joseph. But Joseph wasn't willing to sacrifice his family just because they turned against him. He kept his heart pure, was determined to honor God in the way he lived his life, and refused to be ruled by bitterness. It was his Godly character that made him stand out from the crowd and that ultimately led to his position of power and influence in Egypt. What they all had to acknowledge in the end, was that even though Joseph's brothers meant their actions for evil, God ordained those same events for good. (Gen. 50:20).

So if it seems that your unsaved family members are treating you far worse than you deserve, bear in mind that God is at work on your behalf, and that actions intended to bring you pain and hurt may be the very things God will use to rescue your entire family from sin.

In the end, Joseph had no other desire than that even his remains would be close to his family, that he might forever enjoy with them the promises of God he himself made it possible for them to receive.

### Amram & Jochebed (Moses' Parents)

These are two names we don't hear very often, and even reading through this account in Hebrews 11, it would be easy to overlook them. But if you'll read versc 23 carefully, it is not Moses the text honors, it is his parents. Before we even get to Moses' exploits, it is his parents who are described as having shown faith so distinctive and daring that they are worthy of mention among this revered company.

Their names are not even given, but their faith is to be forever remembered.

Their faith was in their refusal to comply with the evil commandment of Pharaoh, and their willingness to risk everything to save their son—their heritage—from the fate that befell *every other family in Israel.*

Thanks to his parents, and the protecting, guiding hand of God, the baby Moses was carefully directed into the waters near Pharaoh's palace. There his sister awaited her chance to help keep Moses safe:

"Then said his sister to Pharaoh's daughter, Shall I go and call to thee a nurse of the Hebrew women, that she may nurse the child for thee?

"And Pharaoh's daughter said to her, Go. And the maid went and called the child's mother.

"And Pharaoh's daughter said unto her, Take this child away, and nurse it for me, and I will give thee thy wages. And the woman took the child, and nursed it." (Ex. 2:7-9).

What an irony that Moses' mother would be paid wages to nurse her own child—by the daughter of the very person who plotted his death. This was a divinely appointed opportunity to ensure that Moses received training in the Hebrew faith before he was ever introduced to Egyptian education. In his journey to manhood, this was what he would remember. The teaching Moses received at the hand of faithful Jochebed, his own mother, would remain the dominant influence in his heart throughout his life.

The Bible provides the best commentary on this dramatic example of God's providence: "And we know that all things work together for good to them that love God, to them who are the called according to his purpose." (Rom. 8:28).

## *Lessons Never Forgotten*

Every Christian mother reading this should take encouragement from the fact that their Godly influence on their young children is something that will never be forgotten. At times it may appear that our children have turned their back on spiritual things, but, as my own mother used to say, "There's a day after today!" In other words, don't give up. Don't resign yourself to the fact that just because everyone else's child is being claimed "by Pharaoh" that you have to give up yours too. It is not so, for God's Holy Spirit will move in response to your fervent prayers, and bring to mind the lessons you teach your children in their youth. "Train up a child in the way he should go: and when he is old, he will not depart from it." (Pr. 22:6).

This is not to suggest that a child, yielding to their own God-given free will, cannot turn his back on the teachings of his youth and do things that may break his parents' hearts. Of course that can happen, and even to the most careful, Godly parents. It would be easy to send good parents on a "guilt trip" over what they might or might not have done in bringing up their kids, but that wouldn't help anyone. We've all done things we wish we could do over, but my first concern here isn't the past, it is to assure you of hope and help in God for your family's future. Moses' parents refused to give up on their son despite the most dire of circumstances, and we shouldn't give up on our kids either—NOT EVER!

"They shall not labor in vain, Nor bring forth children for trouble; For they shall be the descendants of the blessed of the LORD, And their offspring with them.

"It shall come to pass that before they call, I will answer; And while they are still speaking, I will hear." Is. 65:23,24, NKJV).

### *Free Will Or God's Will?*

Free will or not, a child who has grown up under the influence of loving Christian parents will learn things that he or she will never be able to forget no matter how hard they try. On the subject of free will, there's something important to note about the verse we quoted earlier from Proverbs 22. That phrase, "in the way he should go" may also rendered, "according to his way." In other words, the parent who continually allows a child to have his own way is laying a foundation for self-willed living. If a child learns that lesson in his youth, he certainly "will not depart" from it when he is older, at least not without a great deal of difficulty. That may help explain why good spiritual lessons faithfully taught by parents get set aside in later years, as that strong self-will is asserted more and more often. The lesson here is to "train up" your child by not always allowing him to live "according to his own way." That can become a battle if your young child's temperament keeps pushing him in that direction, and it will almost certainly precipitate the need for discipline and correction. But that's a battle worth fighting, and will help develop in your child a spirit willing to bend to the leading of God who will seek first to follow His will, not his or her own.

## *Moses*

Most Christians will be well acquainted with the story of Moses, and it hardly needs to be said that God used Moses in circumstances that affected many more people than just his own immediate family. The verses here in the "Hall of Faith" make reference to everything from his standing up to Pharaoh to the institution of the Passover and to the Exodus and the miracle at the Red Sea. Moses is arguably the most significant leader the Jewish people have ever had. "And there arose not a prophet since in Israel like unto Moses, whom the LORD knew face to face."(De. 34:10). He led Israel through dark days of slavery and suffering and took them to the borders of the Land of Promise. He was a fearless prophet who never failed to deliver God's Word to Israel. He was the vessel God used to convey His Law to Israel, the same Law which has provided the foundation for the legal and moral codes of civilized society ever since.

And no one's life more beautifully foreshadowed the Lord Jesus, our ultimate Deliverer from the slavery and suffering of sin.

## *Choosing The Promises Of God*

So many significant and miraculous events surrounded Moses' life, but along with all that, the Household Salvation connection still comes through loud and clear. It mattered to Moses who he was known as, and who his family was. Firstly, he "refused to be called the son of Pharaoh's daughter." (He. 11:24). He could well have claimed a place in the line of succession to the throne of Egypt, the most powerful civilization of the day, but his place in that family didn't count nearly as much to him as his place in a family seeking out the promises of God.

Secondly, when Moses asked how he should identify himself as being sent from God, the answer was, "Thus shalt thou say unto the children of Israel, The LORD God of your fathers, the God of Abraham, the God of Isaac, and the God of Jacob, hath sent me unto you: this is my name for ever, and this is my memorial unto all generations." (Ex. 3:15). Moses wasn't the instigator of some new religion. God had already made a covenant with Abraham that had been passed down through the generations to Moses, and now it was Moses' God-given responsibility to ensure that those divine promises would continue to be passed on "to all generations." Moses even named his son Gershom, meaning "a stranger in a strange land," a permanent reminder that this child was born in the desert of Midian, not the Land of Promise. Gershom's name literally means "refugee," and, as Moses began to fulfill God's calling in his life, he would always know that his job would not be complete until his son's unfortunate status was permanently changed. I don't mean to read too much into Moses' choice of his son's name, especially since at the time he chose the name, he had no knowledge of all that would transpire in the years ahead, but it does suggest that Moses was conscious of the need for a better future for his family than seemed likely at the time.

## *A Family Affair*

Moses' family were very much involved in all that happened in his life. Aaron, Moses' brother would be his mouthpiece before Pharaoh and before the children of Israel. His sister, Miriam, the one who had so carefully assisted in the rescue of Moses by Pharaoh's daughter, would also play a role. Despite error that produced serious personal consequences, (she was temporarily smitten with leprosy), she was named in Scripture as one clearly prominent in Israel's history: "For I brought thee up out of the land of Egypt, and redeemed thee out of the house of servants; and I sent before thee Moses, Aaron, and Miriam." (Mi. 6:4). The point is, for all Moses' great responsibilities as a leader of unparalleled significance in Israel, he still cared about his family, still included them, honored them and prayed for them: "And Moses cried unto the LORD, saying, Heal her (Miriam) now, O God, I beseech thee." (Nu. 12:13).

God may have great things in store for you, but no matter how He intends to use you, He makes no demands that you sacrifice your loved ones on the altar of success. Some folks want God to use them to save the world, while their loved ones either never enter their thoughts or do so primarily when they see how to use them to further their own goals. They may not even be conscious of it, but their loved ones certainly are.

I was speaking to a fellow minister the other day, who excitedly told me of the great success he had been having in his meetings. He told me he had just finished a long series of five and ten week revivals and that they'd been having tremendous results. I congratulated him, then asked, "How do your wife and children handle all those long spells when you're away from home?"

His head lowered a little. "We're in the middle of a bitter divorce," he said. I don't mean to be judgmental of my brother, but I just don't believe God wanted this man's family torn apart as the price required for all those "revivals."

If Moses could take time for his family with all that he had going on his life, surely we can. This is not deep theology here, just common sense. If you want to get your family saved, spend time with them, include them in your plans whenever you can, and pray for them often.

## *Rahab*

Rahab could have done several things when the Israelite spies came to her for help. Remember that she was a prostitute who sold herself for money. To her, anything she might have done to improve her financial position would surely have seemed attractive. But she didn't sell out the spies to the king for a reward, nor did she demand payment from them in return for her help. Instead she did two very unexpected things. First, she made a statement of faith:

"And she said unto the men, I know that the LORD hath given you the land, and that your terror is fallen upon us, and that all the inhabitants of the land faint because of you.

"For we have heard how the LORD dried up the water of the Red sea for you, when ye came out of Egypt; and what ye did unto the two kings of the Amorites, that were on the other side Jordan, Sihon and Og, whom ye utterly destroyed.

"And as soon as we had heard these things, our hearts did melt, neither did there remain any more courage in any man, because of you: for the LORD your God, he is God in heaven above, and in earth beneath." (Jo. 2:9-11).

Next, she extracted a promise, not for financial rewards, but for the safety of her family:

"Now therefore, I pray you, swear unto me by the LORD, since I have showed you kindness, that ye will also show kindness unto my father's house, and give me a true token:

"And that ye will save alive my father, and my mother, and my brethren, and my sisters, and all that they have, and deliver our lives from death." (Jo. 2:12,13).

Rather than ingratiate herself with the king of Jericho, she was willing to risk her own life and send him on a wild goose chase. Nothing mattered to her more than that her family would be safe, and that they would be under the protection of a God whom, even in her pagan state, she already recognized as "God in heaven above, and in earth beneath."

Rahab's reward went well beyond deliverance from death for her and her family. By marriage she became a member of the household of Nahshon (Mt. 1:4,5), whose sister Elisheba was married to Aaron (Ex. 6:23). During Israel's travels in the wilderness, Nahshon was assigned first place in the order of Judah's host (Nu. 2:3; 7:12,17; 10:14). Rahab and her husband, Salmon, were the parents of Boaz (Mt. 1:5) who married Ruth. Boaz and Ruth had a son named Obed, who had a son named Jesse, who was the father of David, king of Israel. A pagan prostitute became a shining symbol of God's grace, and was elevated from certain death to an honored place in Israel's history, incorporated into the very lineage of Christ Himself.

## *Your Challenge*

Of the others in the "Hall of Faith," I have to say with the Hebrew writer, "the time would fail me to tell." God is still looking for others like them, people who are willing to put everything on the line to get their families saved, people who are willing to pay any price and become modern-day heroes of faith—Household Salvation heroes!

# Chapter Four

# The Cornelius Criteria

*"And he (Cornelius) showed us how he had seen an angel in his house, which stood and said unto him, Send men to Joppa, and call for Simon, whose surname is Peter;*
*"Who shall tell thee words, whereby thou and all thy house shall be saved."*

(Acts 11:13,14)

Having surveyed centuries of Biblical history in our brief look at Hebrews 11, I think it's fair to say we have already made a good case for the proposition that God moves in families, that He is constantly working to bring entire families to know Him, and that Household Salvation is very much a top priority in the plan of God for each one of us. As we continue to look at what the Bible says about Household Salvation, however, it's important not just to think in terms of what God did for those we read about, but to directly apply the principles we learn from their lives into our own circumstances. In the book of Acts, for instance, we read about one of the early Church's most pivotal characters, Cornelius.

His life provides several key lessons to those striving to win their family members to Christ. It must be stressed again that there is no "magic formula" here, just good Biblical information to be mixed with the ability, strength and wisdom God makes available to each one of us determined to live for Him and do His will!

We first read of Cornelius in Acts, chapter ten, where we learn that he was, "A devout man, and one that feared God with all his house, which gave much alms to the people, and prayed to God alway." (Ac. 10:2). Right away we get a picture of a man who was serious about the things of God, one who backed up his beliefs with tangible acts of kindness and compassion. Even though he was a Gentile—only Jews had thus far been baptized into the Christian faith—he prayed and lived as Godly a life as the knowledge he had allowed. He would become the very first non-Jew to receive Christ (without first converting to Judaism) and he was the forerunner in the revolution Christianity effected on the entire world. The following characteristics displayed by Cornelius represent five important principles you and I need to put into practice if we are going to win our loved ones to Christ:

## 1. He Prayed.

The Scripture says of Cornelius that he "prayed to God alway." The use of the outdated form of the word "always" might distract some into overlooking the degree of dedication Cornelius had to his prayer life. He prayed, according to the meaning of the original text, *continually!* And these were not just ritualistic repetitions; he prayed with such force and devotion that God sent him an angel to respond to those prayers and give him specific instructions. "Thy prayers and thine alms are come up for a memorial before God," the angel assured him (Ac. 10:4). Remember, he was a Gentile, a centurion in the Roman army of all things. Not exactly the material religious minds of the day might have had in mind for one so crucial to the development of the early Church. Now, I know what you're going to read next is going to appear a little simplistic, but indulge me for a moment while a make a short statement that can change your whole life: *PRAYER WORKS!*

It doesn't matter how rich you are, how "important" you are or what job you do, if you'll develop a consistent, genuine prayer life, you can change not only your own life, but that of everyone for whom you take time to pray. I'm not suggesting you can have whatever you want simply by speaking a few words, but I am saying that if you'll get into intimate communion with God, take authority in the Name of Jesus over the powers of darkness and persist in prayer no matter what discouragement circumstances are determined to inflict, *you will make a difference!* Simplistic or not, this is truth much more overlooked than over-exercised and it is key to everything else that happens in the Christian life!

Words form prayers, but prayer is more than words. Prayer is expressed as you live, walk and interact with God and with other people. Prayer is what you really want, whatever the words are that happen to come out of your mouth. That is, if you say in a certain formulation of words that you'd like God to do a certain thing, and then live in a way that expresses a desire for something completely contrary, you've prayed, you've sought and you've strived for that thing, not for what your words may have indicated. If I pray, "God, I don't want my child to go to hell, please save him," but then live a carnal lifestyle myself, never bothering to go to church or giving him any valid spiritual example to follow, I can hardly claim to be serious, even though I may think I've "prayed." We don't need to be perfect for God to answer our prayers, but we do need to understand that effective prayer involves our entire lifestyle, not just the occasional use of our religious vocabulary.

E.M. Bounds said, "What the Church needs today is not more or better machinery, not new organizations or more and novel methods, but men whom the Holy Ghost can use—men of prayer, men mighty in prayer. The Holy Ghost does not flow through methods, but through men. He does not come on machinery, but on men. He does not anoint plans, but men—men of prayer."

If I've learned anything over the years concerning Household Salvation, it's that *NOTHING* happens without prayer. I only have to think of my own family's experience. I am here today because a faithful uncle prayed and won his brothers and their families to Christ. Among those saved was my mother, who then prayed for seven years for my dad's salvation. Dad was as lost in sin as any man can be, but my mother's prayers broke that bondage and Dad didn't only get saved he became a preacher of the Gospel. In his dedication to the things of God, he still sets the example I endeavor to follow in my own life and ministry... All because somebody prayed!

I love this quote by J. Sidlow Baxter: "Men may spurn our appeals, reject our message, oppose our arguments, despise our persons, but they are helpless against our prayers."

Clearly, Cornelius was a man who understood the importance of prayer, so much so that his prayers moved angels into action and set in motion events that changed the world. Who knows what can happen when you pray? Who knows what that presently unsaved loved one of yours can accomplish in the Lord, or whom their testimony will touch in years to come? Prayer is more than just a good idea. It's more than just one of the principles one might choose to mention in a book like this. It's more than just an important weapon in the Christian's spiritual arsenal... *PRAYER IS EVERYTHING!*

## 2. He Gave.

We saw in Acts 10:4 how important Cornelius' prayers were, but God also took account of something else—his giving! "Thy prayers *AND THINE ALMS* are come up for a memorial before God." Alms are a special kind of giving. Alms means charitableness and compassion towards the poor or infirm. When Cornelius gave, it was to those who genuinely needed help. Some folks like to give where they can be noticed and honored or where their "gifts" grant them some kind of influence, but Cornelius simply saw needs and met them because they needed to be met.

I can't explain exactly how it works in the divine order of things, I only know that God honors and blesses people with giving hearts in ways that are much more than just financial or material. I'm deeply committed to my belief that God will honor us financially when we tithe and give offerings, and I fully understand the principles of sowing and reaping, but I would be utterly remiss as a Minister of the Gospel if all I stressed in the realm of giving to God were likely financial blessings. I believe that a willingness to give to God, especially in response to the most basic kind of needs that Cornelius labored to meet, is a truly accurate barometer of our spirituality and openness to the things of God. If we can coldly turn our hearts away from those in our society who most need our help, why should God expect our hearts to warm to anyone else? If we truly desire to see a move of God in our families, and we want God to use us to win them into the Kingdom, such desire will surely also be reflected in our attitudes towards others in need. Cornelius saw the Holy Ghost fall upon his entire family, as well as his "near friends" (see Ac. 10:24,44), but their salvation and blessing would likely never have happened without his compassionate heart and desire for more of God.

Notice that it was praying AND giving that produced such astonishing results. It's obviously vital that we pray, but when we combine those prayers with our giving, we create what Acts 10:4 calls a "memorial." In other words, our prayers and our giving together form a spiritual synthesis so powerful that it has a unique way of making God remember our situation.

Again, I can't explain how it all works, I only know that I've seen it happen in my own life and I've seen it work time and time again in the lives of others. I have a missions burden for Romania, and we've been particularly involved in helping abandoned children who are warehoused in Romania's crumbling orphanage system. People all over the world have joined with our ministry to help by giving "alms" to these poorest of the poor. These are many of the same people who come weeping to the altar in our services, desperate for God to do something in their own families. I tell them unashamedly that as they reach out to help those with no father, no mother, no one else to care for them, they are setting the hand of God in motion in their own circumstances. I can't count the times I've seen those people write or call me or come up to me in a later meeting to tell me incredible Household Salvation testimonies.

Sometimes it only takes days. I know of one woman whose husband was saved the very same night she combined her giving with her praying. An unsaved man who studiously avoided Christian television, this woman's husband found himself transfixed as he came across a preacher of the Gospel on his TV set. He knelt down on his living room floor and accepted Christ—and was saved before his wife even made it home from the meeting!

I repeat, I'm not advocating some "magic formula!" You can't buy the moving of the Holy Spirit and if you give with that kind of motivation you'll get nowhere. But sincere prayer, the "effectual, fervent" prayer of the righteous, that is expressed in the life of a compassionate, love-driven Christian cannot fail to produce eternal results. Let me repeat an earlier quotation: "Men may spurn our appeals, reject our message, oppose our arguments, despise our persons, but they are helpless against our prayers." (J. Sidlow Baxter). Our unsaved loved ones are helpless against our prayers, and utterly defenseless against the combined power of our praying and our giving!

## 3. He Had A Godly Reputation

Acts 10:22 tells us how Cornelius was described to the Apostle Peter: "And they said, Cornelius the centurion, a just man, and one that feareth God, and of *good report* among all the nation of the Jews, was warned from God by an holy angel to send for thee into his house, and to hear words of thee." The "good report" Cornelius enjoyed among the Jewish people clearly sprang from the godly lifestyle we have already discussed. While there's no reason to cover that ground again, it's important to realize that our testimony to those outside will obviously impact our families, especially those who live under the same roof with us. By the same token, don't expect to have a good testimony outside the home if you treat your own family shabbily. You can smile as big as you like in church and say "amen" louder than anyone else, but if you live a half-hearted, carnal life at home, your family will know it, your kids will know it, and your "good report" will be meaningless to them. Eventually, no matter how well you fake it, it will become meaningless to the rest of the world as well.

People can be so careless with their reputation, not worrying about it till they've lost it. By then it may be all but impossible to ever get it back. When Jim Wright resigned as Speaker of the House in the midst of an ethical scandal, he said, "Horace Greeley had a quote that Harry Truman used to like:'Fame is a vapor, popularity an accident, riches take wings, those who cheer today may curse tomorrow, only one thing endures—character.'"

Cornelius had character. His family knew it, his friends knew it, and the people he helped by his generous works of charity knew it. What if he'd soiled his reputation in some way? Perhaps Peter, hearing of some problem or flaw in Cornelius' lifestyle might have decided against going to see him. The entire course of history would have been changed, and it's even possible that you and I might not be enjoying the blessings of salvation today. I have to ask, what do people know of your character? What kind of reputation have you established among those you know waiting to be won to Christ? I ask this question of my own heart as much as of yours, for it is a continuing day-to-day process to guard our reputations, maintain our integrity, and keep short accounts with God. It's all the more important when the ones you want to win to Christ are your own family. They really do see all the faults and failings, up close and personal. That doesn't mean you have to be perfect, but you do have to be genuine. They'll see right through hypocrisy, because they know you. They know how you react to adversity, or whether you deal fairly with them when there's conflict, or whether what you say is really in your heart, or if it's just words. Cornelius succeeded in bringing his entire household and his friends with him into the Kingdom of God in large measure because he had established his character, and they knew he was a man they wanted to follow.

## 4. He Was Obedient

If you want to win your loved ones to Christ, you have to listen to God and then follow His instructions. It sounds simple enough, but you know as well as I that all kinds of things will pop into your mind when it comes to actually putting that theory into practice. As far as witnessing to your family is concerned, all kinds of things can hinder you despite your best intentions to be obedient. You might worry about being embarrassed, or rejected, or perhaps about starting an argument with a particularly cantankerous relative. Cornelius had very straightforward instructions:

"And he showed us how he had seen an angel in his house, which stood and said unto him, Send men to Joppa, and call for Simon, whose surname is Peter;

"Who shall tell thee words, whereby thou and all thy house shall be saved." (Ac. 11:13,14).

Now, admittedly, it's probably easier to carry out instructions from God if they're delivered by an angel. There's not much doubt about the source and there's obviously a certain imperative quality to their pronouncements. However, we don't all need angels to appear to know what God wants us to do. God has already given you "words whereby thou and all thy household shall be saved." The Bible is full of them and it certainly ought to be clear by now that He wants you to start using them and using the tools He has provided to help you win your loved ones into the Kingdom.

You've heard the old cliché that the longest journey starts with the first step. Most of such little sayings only become overused clichés because of one thing—they're true! So don't miss the point: If you want to embark on a journey that leads to your family members coming to Christ, you've got to do one thing right away—start! When the angel gave Cornelius his instructions, he didn't wait till next morning (according to Ac. 10:3, it was already after three o' clock in the afternoon), or some other convenient time, he got things started immediately.

"And when the angel which spake unto Cornelius was departed, he called two of his household servants, and a devout soldier of them that waited on him continually;

"And when he had declared all these things unto them, he sent them to Joppa." (Ac. 10:7,8).

If you haven't already followed the example of Cornelius in terms of your prayer life or your giving or establishing your Christian testimony, it's definitely time to start on those things. Also, in practical terms, one of the most helpful things you can start doing immediately is simply to focus in on those family members you want to win to Christ. You could start with just one of your loved ones and pray a bit longer for him or her. Then do something special for that individual; bake a pie or send flowers or a little "thinking of you" card—anything just to express how much you care and how much you love them. If you haven't done something like that in a while, that's all the more reason to do it right away.

It doesn't need to be anything expensive and it doesn't have to be anything with overtly spiritual overtones. All you're trying to do is show your love and the love of Christ in you, and communicate the Gospel through your life and your actions, not just your words. As you'll see in later chapters, there's a lot more you can begin doing, it's just important that you begin doing something!

## 5. *Cornelius Cared!*

Although we've made the point that Cornelius was a man of compassion, it's important to understand that he was also someone who specifically cared about his own family. Lots of people get so wrapped up in their work and their public duties that they can easily neglect their own folks back at home. Cornelius, however, was a man who went out of his way to include his family:

"And the morrow after they entered into Caesarea. And Cornelius waited for them, and had called together his kinsmen and near friends." (Ac. 10:24).

He could simply have waited, not mentioned anything to anyone and had his meeting with Peter on his own. But something in Cornelius' heart told him that events of extraordinary significance were unfolding, and he wanted his family to be a part of it.

Many times in our ministry I've counseled people who have become perplexed by the attitudes of their unsaved loved ones towards them. To paraphrase one woman's complaint: "He just sits there with his beer and watches TV. No matter how much I pray, he just keeps acting like he always did. Will he ever change?"

This woman had come to Christ, her life had been radically changed and, obviously, she wanted her husband to share in the joy of her newfound spiritual life. However, as I had to point out, her husband was still acting like an unsaved man because he still *was* an unsaved man!

"Put yourself in his position," I told her. "One day, when his life is perfectly normal, and you're completely happy with the way he's living, you go out and 'get religion.' None of the things you used to do together interest you, and now you're so busy going out to church and being with your new Christian friends, or else spending all that time alone in your room praying for him, that he has nothing else he can do except watch TV and drink beer. But he didn't change, *you changed.* He doesn't know what in the world he can do to get on common ground with you.

"You need a plan," I continued. "I want you to make yourself the most exciting woman he's ever met. Shower him with affection and attention. Take him home a huge bunch of flowers, cook him his favorite meal tonight, and make sure it's a night he'll never forget. Then do it all over again tomorrow. If you do this right, he's not going to want to be anywhere except where you are, and he won't give a hoot what's on TV because he'll be too busy wanting to be with you."

That woman came up to me in a church service just a few months later—accompanied by her beaming, born-again husband! Now, I realize that it takes two to make a relationship, and some of your unsaved relatives may be more aggressively resisting your attempts to share the Gospel than this man was, but the effects of unconditional love and genuine care are always considerable. Remember, you are the one who is walking in the light. It's you who is going to be called upon to go the extra mile, not your unsaved loved ones. Is it worth it? I guess that depends how badly you want to see your loved ones saved from eternal Hell and rejoicing with you in Heaven one day.

Caring costs. It's easy for us to say we care; it's a whole different thing to live like we do, especially when it calls for patience and maybe a little sacrifice. Cornelius practiced the art of caring and ended up changing not only his family's situation, but that of the entire gentile world. A little caring, it seems, goes a long way.

To sum up, from Cornelius we learn five principles we can put into practice in our own lives right away that will directly impact our unsaved loved ones:

1) *He Prayed.* Step one to any success in winning souls, whether in a family situation or otherwise.

2) *He Gave.* He combined his praying with his giving in a way that made God take special notice.

3) *He Had a Godly Reputation.* Inside and outside of his home, He demonstrated Godly character.

4) *He Obeyed.* God told him what to do and he did it without hesitation.

5) *He Cared.* He took the time to show how much he cared for his family.

# Chapter Five

## Are All Your Planks in Place?

Earlier we looked a little at the life of Noah, and found that he "prepared an ark to the saving of his house." (He. 11:7). We noted that God's instructions for the construction of the ark were very specific and that Noah followed them precisely. To repeat our earlier point: God wants you and I to "build an ark" for the saving of our households too, and He has given us instructions that are just as specific and every bit as essential as those He gave to Noah.

I can envisage Noah checking down in the belly of the great vessel as the time for God's judgement through the Flood drew near. "It's been 120 years since I put some of those planks in down here. Will it leak? This thing has to be absolutely watertight or we'll all drown!"

As Noah painstakingly checked that everything was exactly as it was supposed to be, he was doing the same thing you and I must do if we want to ensure that our loved ones are kept safe from the judgement to come—he was making sure all his planks were in place!

Every four years in the United Sates as the major political parties prepare for the presidential election, they announce their platform, which is simply a document stating where they stand on important issues. There's always a lot of talk and sometimes a lot of controversy about which "planks" will be included in the party platform. Well, as important as those issues are, the planks, or guiding principles, that you use to determine the spiritual destiny of your family are far more important. I'm interested in political matters and I believe Christians need to be responsible citizens who are involved in the workings of our great democracy, but politics can only go so far. Spiritual problems demand spiritual solutions, and if the problem is to ensure the eternal salvation of your family members, the solution has nothing to do with how good a Democrat or how good a Republican you are. Your family members getting saved and living lives that are honoring to God can only have a positive impact on society, including the political process, but let's not get the cart before the horse. The first set of planks we need to get busy on are those that are vital to building an ark of safety for our families. Let's make sure the following planks are firmly in place as we set about building our ark:

### *Plank One—Your Strategy*

Everybody's situation is different and you need to develop a strategy that is unique to your special circumstances. If you are the sole Christian in your family, your strategy won't be the same as a family group believing together for the one "lost sheep" who still hasn't come to Christ. And, of course, there are as many different possibilities as there are families. Have a plan, write it down somewhere, and let it guide you in your day-to-day efforts to win your loved ones to Christ. God told Habakkuk to, "Write the vision, and make it plain upon tables, that he may run that readeth it." (Ha. 2:2). You need a plan because circumstances sometimes bring delay and discouragement and you need to always be able to remind yourself what your goal is and why you are having to work so hard. "For the vision is yet for an appointed time, but at the end it shall speak, and not lie: though it tarry, wait for it; because it will surely come, it will not tarry." (Ha. 2:3).

You are about the business of winning souls, and "he that winneth souls is wise." (Pr. 11:30). Winning souls takes wisdom, and if that's true in general, it is even more so in a family situation. Building an ark for your family is going to take effort, persistence and a lot of divine help, but the rewards are eternal and, I think you'll agree, worth any sacrifice necessary.

Who is it in your family that you want to come to Christ? Make a list. If I were you, I'd put down this book and do it right now, or as soon as you possibly can before another day goes by. Now, you're going to have to decide on a set time every day when you bring those names to the Lord in prayer. You're probably already praying regularly for your unsaved loved ones, but if not, I urge you to make that commitment right now. After you've made your list, begin to focus on one name in particular. You'll pray for each one, of course, and you need to try to be open to the leading of God's Spirit as He moves to touch any one of those on your list, but first, let Him lead you to one name. If there's just one unsaved member of your immediate family, a spouse, son, daughter, mother or father, there's probably no question who you'll want to start with.

Having picked your first "target," put in some extra time praying just for that person. You'll eventually do this for all the names on your list, so don't worry that you're going to be playing favorites. Pray for all your unsaved loved ones, but begin praying even more for this special one. Get a little picture of him or her and carry it with you all the time. When you're at lunch, or sitting in your car at a red light, or any other time when you have even just a few seconds alone somewhere, use that time to pray. In the course of a day, you could end up spending a lot more time praying for that loved one than you ever thought possible.

When you pray, be specific about what it is you want God to do. Yes, ask Him to save your loved one, but what you're really doing is taking spiritual authority over the enemy's efforts to keep your loved one from coming to Christ. That means binding the demons of hell in Jesus' Name and, by your prayers, preventing them from having influence over the spiritual decisions your loved one makes. If your loved one has a particularly grievous problem in his or her life, let's say it's gambling and it's causing some real heartache and anxiety, deal specifically with that problem. Don't just say, "God, stop him from gambling." You need to call those demons of gambling and greed by name, rebuke them, and consign them back to the pit of hell where they came from—NEVER TO RETURN!

I'm not one of those who believe demons govern every decision people make, even if they do something not particularly honoring to God, but if there are serious problems to be dealt with—sexual immorality, drug abuse, alcoholism, domestic violence—these threaten the family at it's very core, and you can be sure that Satan and his minions are hard at work behind the scenes. If these are the kinds of things threatening your family's spiritual survival, only fervent, overcoming prayer, directed at ending the demonic onslaught faced by your loved one, can ultimately prevail. I don't mean to sound flippant—these are no small problems—but if you really do want to see your loved one set free, God has given you the most effective weapon ever devised, and it's at your disposal the moment you call on His Name! John said, "And every spirit that confesseth not that Jesus Christ is come in the flesh is not of God: and this is that spirit of antichrist, whereof ye have heard that it should come; and even now already is it in the world. Ye are of God, little children, *and have overcome them: because greater is he that is in you, than he that is in the world."* (1 Jo. 4:3,4).

In my earlier book, *It's Time For Household Salvation,* I talk a little bit about how to "resist the devil, and he will flee from you." (Ja. 4:7). God showed me some things that were rather startling to me at the time. I'd always known the enemy was at work trying to keep some of my family members bound in sin, but I actually began seeing the strategy he was using and, armed with that knowledge, was able to counter it in prayer and see those family members come to Christ. I also discovered that resistance (of the devil) is a continual process. You exert resistance until you prevail, not just till you get tired or bored or occupied by some other pastime. If you're out in your yard and the previous owner left a big stake in the ground right where you want to erect your new garden shed, you need to knock it over and get it out of the way. If you push hard at it with your index finger, you're resisting the presence of the stake, but not very well. Maybe if you put your shoulder to it and push as hard as you can, you'll get somewhere, maybe not. You may need to get out the best tool at your disposal and keep at the job till you get the stake loose enough to pull it out of the ground. However you have to do it, if you want that new shed erected, you just have to keep at it till you get that obstacle out of the way. So it is with resisting the devil. He's in the way of your family's salvation and you can't give up opposing his efforts until you have victory in your grasp.

Here are a few synonyms Webster's Dictionary offers for the word resist: withstand, oppose, hinder, check, thwart, baffle, disappoint, obstruct. In case I haven't made myself clear, I want you to WITHSTAND the devil, OPPOSE his efforts, HINDER his endeavors, CHECK his progress, THWART his strategies, BAFFLE his thinking, DISAPPOINT his evil ambitions, OBSTRUCT his schemes—and RESIST him till you beat him once and for all and no more of your loved ones are lost in sin!

I can't tell you which areas are under attack in your family, but you know them, and a successful strategy for winning your loved ones to Christ depends on your rising to the challenge and refusing to give any more ground to the enemy.

Getting back to our list, if you have quite a few names on there, you may want to concentrate your extra efforts on one person for a week at a time, or a month at a time, or you may just decide to stay focused on that one individual until they come to Christ. Again, I can't tell you which way to go, but do decide on what is best in your situation and stick with your plan.

As important as prayer is, while you're spending those extra efforts on that one particular name on your list, you need to do some other things, too. Try to make sure you get to spend some time with that individual. If it's a family member who lives with you, don't just sit there in front of the TV with them, try to make sure you do something where there's some positive interaction. You could go out to dinner together, or find out if there's something on his or her mind about which they could use a sympathetic ear. Maybe there's a special treat you could think of that you know they'd appreciate, like arranging a trip to a ball game or going to a concert. Just find something to do together, and use that time to show love, concern and genuine interest in their opinions and feelings. I don't want you to turn every encounter into a "preaching" session. They have to know that you can give them spiritual direction and help when they're ready for it, but, first, just make sure they know that you really do care, and that your happy to spend time with them on their terms, not just yours. I don't mean that you have to put up with abuse, even if it's just verbal, or stay in an atmosphere that's patently designed to make you uncomfortable, but you can use wisdom to know when you can just "stick around" and let Christ's love quietly flow out of you into that loved one's life. And I can't think of a better time to inwardly pray for someone than when they're right there with you. At a gentle touch on the shoulder as you pass down the hot dogs, or while you're hugging or shaking hands, pray silently right then, and serve notice on the devil that his time is up in this precious loved one's life.

If you decide that it's time to move on to another family member with your extra efforts in prayer and time spent, don't just forget the ones you've already been working on. Make sure you at least call them regularly, and be ready to respond to anything that seems like either an emergency or a spiritual opportunity.

The whole point is that you sit down and look at your time, and make a conscious effort to block off periods when you concentrate on doing nothing else but reaching your loved ones for Christ. Let God guide you in what specific things you can do, but if you don't get some of these things on to your schedule, you may never do them. It's amazing how much time we can find to devote to things that we enjoy, whether it's watching a favorite TV program or going out with friends or whatever. There isn't anything necessarily wrong with those things, but they may be demanding a higher proportion of your time than you realize. You have two all-important things to make time for—pray for your loved ones, and spend time with them reflecting the love and compassion of Christ.

## *Plank Two—Your Influence*

You need to know certain things about how being a Christian can actually impact your other family members' lives. Did you know that scientific evidence indicates Christians live longer, healthier lives, that they can be statistically shown to be more successful in their professional lives and that they pass on their most deeply held values more effectively (particularly to their children) than others?

As a Christian, you are part of a God-blessed group that, statistically, just does better in important areas of life than non-Christians. I don't mean to suggest that Christians don't have challenges and problems to overcome, but, as a whole, they have tremendous advantages. Generally speaking, problems like physical and mental illness, suicides, drug and alcohol abuse, family instability and more don't afflict Christ-centered families and individuals nearly as badly. And when some of these problems do encroach into a Christian's life, with God's help, they have the means to cope far better than most.

In the business world, there have been studies done that reveal some startling information. Of 1361 corporate vice-presidents questioned, 89% claim to be active Christians, 87% were still married to their original spouse, and 92% were from two-parent families. 91% of CEO's surveyed claimed church affiliation. I mention this only to make the point that there are a lot of things about being a Christian that give you tremendous advantages and opportunities to influence your family members. Being a Christian isn't about "giving up" things to "get religion." Apart from the eternal benefits, it's about living an abundant life filled with noble, God-given expectations, and fulfilling your potential for making a valuable difference in the lives of those around you. If those things aren't appealing to your family-members, I don't know what else could be, and your challenge is to reflect the joy, strength and serenity that makes the Christian life so worth living.

## Plank Three—Your Foundation For The Future

You could say that the points just discussed are areas of "horizontal" influence, things that happen in the lives of Christians that make them stand out in the eyes of others around them, including family members. But there are areas of "vertical" influence, too, things passed down that will have an impact on entire generations not even born yet. Obviously, before you can reach future generations, you have to start with the children you have now. If you don't have kids, or don't have any yet, there are still children and young people in your sphere of influence you can help reach for Christ, but let's start with a few facts for Christian parents. I heard the following statistics cited in a recent sermon: When Mom and Dad go together regularly with their children to church (not just drop them off), 76% of those kids follow on and commit their lives to Christ. When only Dad takes the kids to church, 55% follow. If only Mom takes the kids, the number drops to 15%, and if neither parent takes the kids to church, only 9% will be likely to make decisions for Christ. Abraham Lincoln said, "There is just one way to bring up a child in the way he should go, and that is travel that way yourself."

The Bible teaches us the importance of generational thinking in literally hundreds of instances. King David, for example, had this to say: "But the mercy of the LORD is from everlasting to everlasting upon them that fear him, and his righteousness unto children's children." (Ps. 103:17). The Hebrew word translated here as children is also rendered in other places in Scripture as "son." This word, "ben," is actually taken from the word "banah" meaning "to build." The idea being conveyed is that one builds the family name. In other words, one works towards establishing the family and passing down not just the name, but all the wealth and blessing that goes along with it. That also applies in the realm of salvation—God absolutely intends that you pass along the blessings of salvation to your offspring! Without question, every child needs to make his or her own individual decision to follow Christ, but you, as parents, play the major role in ensuring that the groundwork for making the right decision is carefully laid. You can "build" your family a future in Christ; in other words, you can build them an ark, plank by plank.

"Know therefore that the LORD thy God, he is God, the faithful God, which keepeth covenant and mercy with them that love him and keep his commandments *to a thousand generations.*" (De. 7:9).

If you'd like to do an intriguing word study, get out a concordance and look up words like "generation" or "children" or "family" or "son(s)." You'll find a total of 4,351 references to those words alone. It may be the ultimate in understatement to say that winning your family to Christ is definitely Scriptural!

Earlier, we mentioned Moses, and how important the influence of his mother must have been. That's true, and the old adage that "the hand that rocks the cradle rules the world," is one to which I definitely subscribe. However, I'm going to make a statement now which, in the "enlightened" nineties, some might find a little controversial: As important as the role of the mother is, it is the father who primarily determines the degree of spiritual influence exerted upon children. Now, there are single moms out there, and mothers with unsaved husbands who just started howling at me. They are working hard to bring their kids up for the Lord and I don't for one second want to discourage them. But, ladies, I'm only talking about how things were designed to be. I know you can win out in your situation, and I've dedicated my life to providing support to those dealing with exactly the problems you face. Not that it will be any comfort to you, but there are a lot of homes where the supposedly Christian dad is often "AWOL," too when it comes to bringing up the kids for the Lord. So many moms have to do double the work, making up for the things Dad doesn't do in the spiritual realm.

The fact remains, however, that God designed the family to have at it's head a man who would take the responsibility of being the "priest," or spiritual authority in his household and who, out of his own relationship with God and his study of the Scriptures, would be the chief source of spiritual guidance for the family. Look again at those statistics we cited earlier regarding the effects on children when the father isn't involved in bringing the kids to church. When Dad and Mom take the kids to church, 76% of kids will follow on and make a decision for Christ. When it's Mom alone, the number sadly falls to only 15%. Mom, if you are one of those fighting that battle alone for the souls of your kids, your job is a harder than it ought to be, but let me make it clear that God has provided you, too, with the tools to come out on the winning side of that equation. I can't argue with the statistics, but I can promise you God's help in your circumstances, and I know that His promises concerning Household Salvation are to you as well as to any other family.

Dad, I can't tell you how important your role is. Dr. James Dobson said this: "A team of researchers wanted to learn how much time middle-class fathers spend playing and interacting with their small children. First, they asked a group of fathers to estimate the time spent with their one-year-old youngsters each day, and received an average reply of fifteen to twenty minutes. To verify these claims, the investigators attached microphones to the shirts of small children for the purpose of recording actual parental verbalization. The results of this study are shocking: The average amount of time spent by these middle-class fathers with their small children was thirty-seven seconds per day! Their direct interaction was limited to 2.7 encounters daily, lasting ten to fifteen seconds each! That, so it seems, represents the contribution of fatherhood for millions of America's children."

You don't need me to tell you that's not good enough. I heard a preacher say recently, "If you don't have a godly heritage, start one." Dad, you have the opportunity to affect entire generations to come, not only in your own family, but in all the families who might one day be touched through the testimony of your children and their children and on far into the future. You may pass from this life, but you can make a difference in this world that, literally, need never cease. Some men seek a kind of immortality, whether through their achievements, their wealth or whatever. You can have it by passing on that Godly heritage to your kids and, by your example, teaching them to do likewise.

Gospel musician Hilding Halverson told of overhearing a conversation between his son and two other little boys. The youngsters were bragging about their dads. One boy said proudly, "My dad knows the mayor of our town!" Another said, "So, my dad knows the governor of our state!" Halverson's son then came up with this touching comment, "That's nothing—my dad knows God!" Upon hearing this, Halverson quickly slipped away to his room and with tears in his eyes said, "O God, I pray that my boy will always be able to say,'My dad knows God.'" He knew he had been paid the supreme tribute.

The Bible says, "And, ye fathers, provoke not your children to wrath: but bring them up in the nurture and admonition of the Lord." (Ep. 6:4). The instruction here is to ensure your children are spared the wrath of God by exposing them to godly "training" (according to the Greek word "paideia," used here) and education. The word "nouthesia" translated as "admonition" is referring to discipline. A fuller rendering of the original Greek is "to put in mind," that is, you have to make sure your kids "get it." And, such is the nature of kids, you may have to make sure they get it by using more than just your words sometimes.

Dad, you need to be fully involved in the area of discipline—you can't leave that to Mom alone. If there's a lack of discipline, or if Mom and Dad don't present a united front in matters of discipline, you will be denying your kids a basis for learning the all-important lesson of self-control; and if they can't learn that, I'm not sure they can really learn anything.

None of this means you can indulge in harsh, callous or unfair treatment of your children. God's Word is very clear: "Fathers, don't scold your children so much that they become discouraged and quit trying. (Col. 3:21, TLB). Nevertheless, you do need to take responsibility for disciplining your children if you truly desire a victorious and meaningful life for them as they grow older. I suppose we could have made the subject of discipline one of our "planks" in its own right, it's that important. It is an indispensable component of the ark you build for the future safety and spiritual well-being of your family. And remember, we're not just talking about the family living under your roof today.

You are laying a foundation for future generations, too. What your kids don't learn, they can't pass on to their kids, and that may affect the future in ways you can't possibly imagine. Decades from now, should the Lord tarry, someone you'll never know—or maybe lots of "someones"—may well be won to Christ because of the foundation you lay in your family today.

## Plank Four—Spread The Table

This is where building your ark starts to get exciting. There's not a whole lot of "deep" teaching that goes with this, but it's an important point to make. When your loved ones start getting hungry for God, you need to be prepared with the spiritual food they're looking for. In other words, you have to know your subject: "Study to show thyself approved unto God, a workman that needeth not to be ashamed, rightly dividing the word of truth." (2 Tim. 2:15). If one of your loved ones came to you today and asked for spiritual help, could you really give it to them. I know you could pray with them, but could you point them to the Scriptures that deal with salvation, or healing, or deliverance, or whatever their need might be. You've heard about "The Roman Road" and other little selections of Bible verses that can be used to help someone as they are led to Christ. There are lots of ways of presenting the plan of salvation, but are you familiar with one? Could you sit down with a loved one right now and lead them through a clear, simple, Scriptural presentation of what it means to be saved? How about explaining what it means to be filled with the Holy Spirit? Maybe they're interested in the Rapture or something else to do with the end times. Perhaps they want to know what the Bible has to say about Water Baptism. You don't need to hit them with a full-blown theological treatise, and don't forget that your first priority, after all, is not to distract them or impress them with how much you know, but to get them to commit their lives to Christ. You should, however, be reasonably familiar with the biblical basis for the things you believe if you hope to be persuasive in sharing those beliefs with others. Again, it must be stressed, you don't need to try to deliver the entire history and doctrine of Christianity in one sitting, and you certainly don't want to get embroiled in arguing over different doctrinal opinions. Just be sure you know how to lead your loved ones to Christ and how to give them a good start on the incredible journey ahead of them as they begin walking with the Lord.

If you're not equipped to be a soulwinner, it's time to get equipped. Talk to your pastor and ask him to help you at least be prepared to present the plan of salvation. Or get any one of the many good books on soulwinning you'll find at your Christian bookstore. I realize that many reading this will already be prepared in this area, but in the event that you're not, don't put it off another day. It's not particularly difficult, and as you discipline yourself to the study of God's Word, it's not only your loved ones who'll benefit, you will too.

As we've said, there are many ways of presenting the Gospel, and I'd urge you to find a plan that you're comfortable with. If you like, you could start by talking about the following verses with the person you're witnessing to:

"But what does it say?'The word is near you, in your mouth and in your heart' (that is, the word of faith which we preach):

"that if you confess with your mouth the Lord Jesus and believe in your heart that God has raised Him from the dead, you will be saved.

"For with the heart one believes unto righteousness, and with the mouth confession is made unto salvation.

"For the Scripture says,'Whoever believes on Him will not be put to shame.'

"For there is no distinction between Jew and Greek, for the same Lord over all is rich to all who call upon Him.

"For 'whoever calls on the name of the LORD shall be saved.'" (Ro. 10:8-13, NKJV).

After you talk a little bit about what these verses mean (remember, keep it simple, don't get sidetracked and don't get tricked into having an argument), you could point out what it is that stands in the way of any of us having a relationship with the Lord:

"For all have sinned and fall short of the glory of God." (Ro. 3:23, NKJV)

Be sure to point out that you aren't any "better" than they are, you've just been forgiven, and they can be, too. Next, show that the "sin problem" was solved by Christ's sacrifice on Calvary:

"But God demonstrates His own love toward us, in that while we were still sinners, Christ died for us." (Ro, 5:8, NKJV)

As you feel the Holy Spirit moving on his or her heart, you could go back to Ro. 10:9 and "close the sale" as it were. Give them the opportunity to "believe in their heart" and "confess with their mouth" as you lead them in the prayer of salvation.

Everyone is going to have a different approach and you obviously need to use whatever works for you. If you don't have something else to use yet, just talking about these last few verses may serve you well in the meantime.

So "spread the table" in your household, and prepare yourself to provide a spiritual feast that can be ready at a moment's notice. I pray you'll need it soon!

I know this is simple stuff, and if you know all this already, I'm thrilled and I trust you'll enjoy greater success than ever in your future soulwinning efforts. It's just that the Gospel has never been anything but simple, and on the point of leading someone into the Kingdom of God, we need to keep it that way. Don't use "spiritual-sounding" language that can sound downright scary to an unsaved person. They don't know what you mean when you start talking about, "Are you washed in the blood of the

Lamb?" or some of the other esoteric phrases we Christians like to invoke like some sort of secret code. Talk like that to most unsaved people and they'll most likely decide they have enough problems of their own and they don't need any of yours. Just talk like a human being who thinks and feels like they do and who genuinely cares about what's happening in their lives.

We've been talking about "planks," and perhaps you can think of a few others you'd like to have in place as you build that ark for the saving of your household. Go ahead and nail them in; your family's eternal safety may well depend on it!

*Note:* Many thanks to my pastor, Rev. Michael Rippy of Evangel Temple in Montgomery, Alabama for some of the statistics and information used in this chapter.

# Chapter Six

# Household Salvation–
# Church Growth Dynamite

*"Bear ye one another's burdens, and so fulfil the law of Christ."*

(Gal. 6:2)

As an evangelist, I've had the privilege of ministering in countless churches across America, and, almost universally, there is an overwhelming desire among each church's leadership to increase the numbers of people attending their services. Naturally! That's a wonderful desire and a Godly ambition! Some people will say "numbers don't count," and instead assert that it's spiritual growth that matters, not numerical growth. Obviously, I don't disagree with the need for spiritual growth, but, if you'll indulge me for a moment, let's take for granted that every pastor in America who wants his congregation to grow in numbers also wants those added numbers to consist of spiritually mature, teachable, hungry-for-God Christians. It's clearly a good thing to have more people attending our services than less. I have heard of a few folks who wouldn't agree with that, but I have trouble understanding their somewhat curious point of view. God wants us to win the world to Christ, and why any Christian would want anyone else excluded from the Gospel's reach and influence is way beyond me. According to Donald McGavran, it's something we need to think carefully about: "If top priority is not given to effective evangelism by our churches, in two generations the church in America will look much like its counterpart in Europe." The figures he cites, in terms of percentages of population claiming church attendance look like this: United States, 43%; Netherlands, 27%; the former West Germany, 21%; Great Britain, 14%; France, 12%; Sweden, 5%; Finland, 4%; Denmark, 3%.

If you have any heart for God at all, those figures will scare you at least a little. Let's assume, then, that numerical growth in our churches is a good thing. So, if we truly desire an explosion of church growth, what is the best way to bring it to pass? There are plenty of theories on the subject, and I've lost count of the number of Church Growth seminars I've heard about. All of that is wonderful, and I'd encourage everyone to get as much education on this subject as you can, but let me add a little theory of my own into the mix: The number one source of new members for your church is to be found among the families of those already attending every Sunday!

If every member of the congregation of which you are a part, including you, were to win one family member to Christ in the next twelve months, what kind of difference would that make in your church? Firstly, you would have doubled the size of your church within a year. That would be quite an achievement, don't you think? Everywhere I go, that's the challenge I'm issuing to pastors and congregations: "You can double the size of this church within a year!"

Think about it. Next Sunday, when you're worshiping along with your brothers and sisters in Christ, take a look around and ask yourself what effect it would have on your church if there were twice as many people there. Would it make a difference as to how effective your church could be in your community? Wouldn't there be more resources to call upon to get those things done that never seem to get done now? There would be more people giving more time and more money, telling more people about Christ, sending more missionaries around the world and having more of an impact on more lives than you could possibly imagine! Beyond that, what kind of effect would it have on the families in your congregation if their loved ones started coming to Christ in unprecedented numbers? Would it be a positive thing? You'd better believe it! Conflicts would diminish, spirits would lift, anxieties would shrink and joy would break out all over the place. Church would never be the same again!

"Point taken," you say, "but what do I do about it?"

You could start, of course, by doing everything you can to win even just one of your family members to Christ within the next year. I trust this book has already given you some help and encouragement on that point, but that's only the beginning. What if you got together with your fellow congregation members and made Household Salvation a church-wide priority? In other words, you wouldn't just be working towards getting your own family saved, you would be helping others in your church win their families; in turn, they'd be helping you win yours.

Clearly, you can support one another in prayer. Ask God to help you find a prayer partner, a "Household Salvation Partner," within the congregation, then exchange a photo of an unsaved loved one with them and take time to pray not just for your own family but for theirs. Earlier, we talked about focusing on one particular member of your family for special prayer and other efforts. While you're doing that, wouldn't it be wonderful to have someone else agreeing with you in prayer specifically for the loved one you yourself are concentrating on? According to the words of Jesus it would be:

"Again I say unto you, That if two of you shall agree on earth as touching any thing that they shall ask, it shall be done for them of my Father which is in heaven." (Mt. 18:19).

You would certainly want to take every opportunity to meet together somewhere for prayer, but you would also have the comfort of knowing that even when you and your prayer partner are not together, in those busy moments of life when you can't pray, someone else can—just as you can for them.

Some churches in which I've ministered have created a "Household Salvation Wall" in their church. Members bring photographs of unsaved loved ones to place on the wall where they can be prayed for daily by other members of the congregation. The results in some cases have been staggering. Individual fellowships across the country are winning hundreds of souls to Christ, one Brooklyn church doubling in size to six-hundred members within eight months.

When you are working out your strategy for reaching your own family members, you can strengthen that strategy by incorporating the efforts of your "Household Salvation Partner." Simple things like having a cup of coffee together with your prayer partner and the loved one you're praying for can be very effective. Sometimes, your partner's more objective eyes will see things in your relationship with your loved that you can't see—just as you'll be able to do for them. Perhaps they'll notice something you are saying or doing to hinder your soulwinning efforts that you are simply not aware of. I don't think you should necessarily try to turn those little coffee meetings into "preaching sessions," but sometimes your partner will be able to say things you might not be comfortable saying, even it's just to invite your loved one to church next Sunday morning. If you can, though, just let a natural friendship develop between your Household Salvation Partner and your loved one. Do that, and you're already well on the way to some terrific "new" opportunities to present the Gospel—and to win that loved one to Jesus. And don't forget that you have the obligation to try to be a friend to your prayer partner's loved ones as well!

Just the fact that you'll be able to share your concerns with someone of like mind is so important; that can really ease your anxieties if things in the family start getting a little rough.

Obviously, before you can begin any kind of church-wide self-evangelization program—and that's what this is—you need your church leadership to be involved. You don't need anyone's permission to ask a fellow church member to pray with you for your family, but if you want an organized effort that gets an entire congregation excited and motivated, it simply can't be done without the guidance and counsel of your pastor and his staff.

Some people might already know who they'd like for a Household Salvation prayer partner, but others won't, and it will take someone in leadership who knows the congregation well to put the right people together. Your church also provides the support structure you need to help you deal with some of the problems that may arise after you start seriously focusing on your family's salvation. For instance, your church can organize special Bible Studies on the subject of Household Salvation, which can be invaluable both as a training tool and as a means to encourage folks who are having a tough time at home. (Note: Our ministry has created a six-week "Household Salvation Video Bible School" that church groups can study together for this very purpose.)

Another thing I encourage churches to do is have a "Salvation Sunday" several times a year. As you know, there are several months in the year that have five Sundays. On the fifth Sunday of each such month, a church can make a special day when the efforts of the entire congregation are focused on getting people to church who need to be saved. That day, the pastor preaches a straight-down-the-line evangelistic sermon geared primarily at winning souls. The songs the choir and others sing are salvation songs, the praise and worship is seeded with the Gospel message, and special testimonies are given where the power of God's saving grace is clearly demonstrated.

Obviously, those are definitely days you want to make sure your unsaved loved ones are at church with you. If you don't feel sure about inviting them yourself, your "Household Salvation Partner" can help you out, and you can do the same for them. You could organize a special Sunday dinner with your partner, and invite your unsaved loved ones to attend after church. That way your invitation could sound something like, "Tom's wife is planning for you and I to eat out (or whatever the eating arrangements are) with them after church this Sunday. If you can't come that's fine, but if we tell her you're coming and then we don't turn up with you, we'll be in big trouble. It's okay if you can't make it, but we need to let her know one way or the other."

You can alter the invitation any way you like to suit the circumstances, but the point is, you need to get that loved one to make a concrete decision. If you leave them saying, "Well, I'll try to make it," there's a pretty good chance you won't see them, so give them a reason to make their mind up. An invitation like this is definitely worth making whether it's Salvation Sunday or not, but if you can be certain the salvation message will be clearly presented, so much the better. Once again, the important thing here is to start thinking strategically, being "wise as serpents and harmless as doves." (Mt. 10:16). If you have a plan you can work towards its completion; if you don't, you simply have a dream that may or may not come pass, but you may end up being more of a hindrance than a help.

If you find that your pastor or your church leadership don't want to pursue things exactly the way I've suggested, whatever you do, don't get upset about it. They have a job to do and they know the parameters that govern their particular situation. I thank God every day that I'm an evangelist, not a pastor, because their job looks to me like the hardest one on earth. I definitely don't want to tell them how to do their jobs, because there's a huge possibility that they know some things I don't. Just make sure you do all that you can do within whatever guidelines your pastor and leadership are comfortable with and you will still end up accomplishing a lot more than you would have otherwise.

Having said that, with all due deference to the calling and anointing on the lives of my pastor friends, I want to issue this challenge to everyone—pastor, staff member, board member, elder, deacon, or the person who just started attending church the other week: Make your church an indispensable part of the Household Salvation strategy of every member of your congregation. And if they don't seem to have a strategy, help them get one.

Pastor, your church can become a magnet for everyone in your community who is serious about winning his or her family members to Christ. However, I know how hard it can be when you're the one balancing all the demands your job places on you, and then to have this guy-with-the-big-ideas evangelist start telling you to "double your church within a year!" I can only say that I've seen it happen, I've dedicated my life to helping make it happen as often as I possibly can, and I've promised God that I'll do everything in my power to assist every pastor and every church member make it a reality right where they are. Obviously, I can't personally visit every church in America, which is why our ministry has worked so hard to develop support materials, books, audio cassettes, videos, study guides and more. This thing has consumed me. As an evangelist, I've always been interested in winning souls, and God has graciously allowed our ministry to help win many thousands over the years. But this is way beyond what one evangelist can accomplish, no matter how many services he conducts or how many television shows he produces. This is a way to unleash the soul-winning potential of every member of your congregation and join them together in a cause dear to every one of their hearts. Getting everyone in your congregation excited about Household Salvation will set off an explosion of church-growth dynamite that will impact your city and the families in your church for years—no, for generations—to come!

# Chapter Seven

# The Father's Heart

*"And he arose, and came to his father. But when he was yet a great way off, his father saw him, and had compassion, and ran, and fell on his neck, and kissed him."*

(Lu. 15:20)

When Jesus told the story we know as "The Prodigal Son," He did not intend His listeners to focus primarily on the son and his misadventures, but on the father and the boundless well of compassion that sprang from his heart. Of course, Jesus wanted us to understand that it is God's heart which is so full of compassion and longsuffering towards each one of us, and He remains every bit as willing to receive a fallen sinner back into the household of faith as the prodigal's father was to welcome home his son. If you've ever felt unworthy, or felt like a failure, this story is surely the ultimate encouragement and reminder of God's unconditional love. It is also a perfect illustration of the lengths God is willing to go to redeem that lost loved one you're so concerned about. No matter how distant your loved one's "far country" is, God can dictate the circumstances needed to press them harder than they've ever been pressed, and provide them opportunity to repeat the Prodigal's experience and "come to themselves."

There's so much in this story, but if there's one thing that stands out to me as a father, it is that God understands exactly how I'd feel if one of my kids went the way of the prodigal. God is our Heavenly Father. We, His children, His creation—and I must sadly include even those of us who have declared our faith in the Lord Jesus Christ—so often turn from His will to pursue our own wants and pleasures. In some cases, the error is quickly corrected and may cause no real lasting damage, but I don't doubt that everyone reading this can point with deep regret to some time in their life when they have succumbed to selfishness and rebellion. I don't make this point to make you feel bad, but to demonstrate why God can relate so precisely to our own feelings. When one of our loved ones is consumed by his or her personal agenda, utterly given over to sin and worldly pursuits, and we begin to feel anxiety, even heartbreak, and the pain of the situation is almost too much to bear—God knows exactly what you're going through. He's been there. He has suffered that same sense of disappointment, and He has had to stand aside in agonizing self-restraint, allowing His children to go on hurting Him until they see the pig-pen for what it is and turn, at long last, back towards home... back towards Him. I've said this many times: If you think you're concerned about your loved ones and their eternal destiny, you're not nearly as concerned as God is.

## *Identifying With God The Father*

In many ways, it's hard for me to identify with the majesty and the omnipotence and the awesomeness of such a great and holy God. It's amazing to think that a being so powerful that He spoke an entire universe into existence could operate on a level with which I can even begin to relate. Yet, in this one area, that of a father concerned and full of love for his child, I can see His thoughts and know His heart. In a sense, God and I can sit around the table and talk about this point on the same level. Before we return to the story of the prodigal and his father, stop and think for a moment of what it must have been like that day on Calvary, when a God who could have sent legions of angels to rescue His only begotten Son from the cross, who could have eradicated Christ's tormentors in seconds, instead turned His back and allowed His Son to bear the burden of sin for all mankind. "This is my beloved Son in whom I am well pleased," He had said; yet the depth of His love for you and me was such that He allowed the brutal horror of Calvary to continue unhindered. Did it cause Him pain to see His Son endure such torture? You know it did. Would you have stopped your child from going through something like that if you had the power to prevent it? There human love and divine love part company,

I think. If that had been my boy, I'd have done anything, fought anyone, endured anything, to save him that awful experience. But, God, who is love, who knows more of love than I could ever hope to, allowed His own Son to suffer... for you... for me... for that spouse or son or daughter or mom or dad or brother or sister... or any other loved one upon your heart, even those lost and struggling somewhere in that "far country" right now.

The entire Gospel story reveals a God determined to speak to us in language we can readily understand. Most of us can't relate very well to a King in a majestic palace, so He was born in a stable. Most of us aren't gifted intellectuals or learned theologians, so He demonstrated the principles of the Kingdom through simple stories, we call them parables, about things like lost sheep and lost coins and wayward sons. And in this parable, we see in the prodigal's father a man with whom we can all identify. Even if you aren't a parent, it's likely that there is someone in your life who could put you through the same emotional torment as the prodigal's father if they were to act as heartlessly as this boy initially did.

Yes, there's much we may never fully understand until we reach Heaven. Even the Apostle Paul said, "For now we see through a glass, darkly; but then face to face: now I know in part; but then shall I know even as also I am known." (1 Cor. 13:12). But for all the mysteries that may remain until that day, the love of the Father is no mystery at all. In this one story, we not only see the incredible depth of God's love for you and me, we also understand that God knows exactly the pain we feel over our lost loved ones, for He feels that way over every single sinner who hasn't yet made his or her way home to Him.

## *When A Loved One Doesn't Love You Back*

Can you imagine how shocked and hurt the prodigal's father must have been that day when his boy came and demanded his share of the inheritance? A hard blow between the eyes from a prowling stranger wouldn't have stunned that father one bit more than what his own son did to him. Jewish law provided that where there were two sons, the eldest was to receive two-thirds of the father's estate while the remaining one-third was given to the youngest son. It wasn't particularly unusual for an older man to divide his wealth among his children before he died, but the way in which the young man demanded "his" portion tells us a lot about the rebellious, selfish mode in which he was operating. It must have been a sizeable inheritance, too. The biblical account indicates that the father was a wealthy man with property, servants and livestock.

This father, like many of us might have done, could have become deeply angry and refused point-blank to give any of his hard-earned wealth to such an obnoxious, ungrateful son. According to Jewish law, he would even have been justified in punishing his son in the most extreme way possible: "And they shall say unto the elders of his city, This our son is stubborn and rebellious, he will not obey our voice; he is a glutton, and a drunkard. And all the men of his city shall stone him with stones, that he die: so shalt thou put evil away from among you; and all Israel shall hear, and fear." (De. 21:20,21).

But such a response, however understandable, wouldn't have given this father what he wanted most. All he cared about was finding a way to get his son to come to his senses, and to do that, he knew he first had to let the boy go. What wisdom he showed. What restraint it must have taken as, full of grief and heartache, he measured out the portion of money demanded by his son. He had worked all his life to accumulate this sizeable fortune and he knew his foolhardy son was about to waste every penny of it, yet still he complied with the boy's wishes. This all might seem a bit contrary to some of the things we've said in this book. "Don't give up on them," you said. Back on page such and such you said, "Don't allow Satan to have his way in their lives." I can assure you, though, that giving up on his son was the last thing on this father's mind.

There does come a time when you know that nothing you say or do is going to change a loved one's mind about their actions, even when you know it's only going to bring them sorrow and possibly years of suffering and regret. In the prodigal's case, a wise father knew that if he made an angry confrontation out of the situation, something might be said or done that would result in the boy never coming back. At all costs, this father was determined not to let that happen. He knew he would never change the boy's mind anyway, and that it was time for Dad to let go. But, as you and I know, that was far from being the end of the story.

Off the boy went to a life that his dad knew would be filled with hard-drinking, sexual immorality and wasteful, selfish excess. I can imagine Dad laying his head on the pillow that first night after the boy left, tears washing down his grief-twisted face. Sobbing long into the night as he prayed and anguished over his boy, a father prepared himself for a long, lonely vigil. I can imagine him as he got up the next morning and began a completely new daily routine. He made his way down to the end of the road to his property and began searching the horizon, hoping beyond hope to see his boy coming back home. Before he went to bed that night, probably waiting till the last of the sunlight disappeared, he did the same thing. The next day he did the same. Then the next day... and the next... and every other day after that.

## Dealing with Guilt

Perhaps, as he stood there for hours peering into the distance, he did what you and I might do. Perhaps he began to tell himself that he should have done better, should have paid more attention to the boy. Who knows what guilt he might have felt as he tortured himself over his "failure" as a parent. It's a natural enough reaction, but it's quite misplaced and potentially soul-destroying. Not that apportioning blame helps in such a situation, but if there is anyone to blame here, it wasn't Dad, it was his impulsive, hot-headed boy.

I have to tell you that, as much as I believe in Household Salvation and the promises of God for your entire family, you are not responsible for, nor can you simply eliminate, the consequences of the choices your loved ones make in life. God can most certainly "restore the years that the locust has eaten" (Joel 2:25), but if a loved one does live among the locusts for a while, some rather precious things are likely to be eaten. It must also be said that some consequences of sin can never be erased. God can forgive and restore someone in the sense that their soul is saved and their eternal destination assured, but they may still have to deal with the natural repercussions of their actions. If someone breaks the law, for example, they will likely still have to deal with the authorities, no matter how genuine their subsequent conversion might be. This father knew that his son would get in all kinds of trouble, and there was no way he could save the boy from the pain ahead. Dad might not have specifically known there was a pig-pen coming, but he knew that whatever it was was bad. Some things your unsaved loved ones do would likely turn your stomach if you knew, but if you only focus on what they're doing or wallow in self-condemnation over what you might or might not have done to prevent the situation, you can't help them and you may do yourself a great deal of emotional harm.

If you do what you can do in terms of making Christ the head of your home, bringing up your kids to love the Lord, and living your life as a genuine, Godly example before them, and they still choose to try out the "far country," you didn't fail, they did. I don't know any perfect people which means I don't know any perfect parents. Yes, you'll make mistakes, we all do. But those mistakes, particularly when made in the context I just mentioned, cannot provide anyone in your family with justification for turning their back on God. Guilt in such a circumstance is a very natural reaction, but it's so important that you don't let it cloud your view of the realities of the situation, nor allow it to discourage you and hamper your faith and determination to pray that loved one back home. Some will say there's no guarantee that they'll ever come home, and in the strictest sense, your loved ones do have the power to make that decision. But I don't think the prodigal "came to himself" by accident, and with all my heart I believe that your love and your prayers can move the hand of God, no matter how many miles away your loved one is, or how far distant their heart may presently be. No, you can't make their choices for them, and you can't force them to come home no matter how much you'd like to, but you can never give up on them either—no matter what!

The prodigal's father certainly never gave up, and, don't forget, what Jesus was showing us was a picture of our Heavenly Father's heart. Every day, Dad went down to the end of the road and began looking for his boy, always waiting, always hoping, always expecting.

## *Life In The Fast Lane—Temporary At Most*

The moment the prodigal left home, one thing was inevitable. He'd waste every dime he had and he'd end up penniless. He found no comfort in any of the "friends" he made before his money ran out. The Bible expresses his situation in words far more telling than any I could write: "He began to be in want." His predicament became so dire he had to endure the most vile humiliation imaginable to any Jew—he took a job feeding pigs. Not only did he have to feed the pigs, things got so bad he was glad of any opportunity to share the slops they ate. Every shred of pride, dignity and self-respect was stripped from him. At that point, wallowing among the pigs, there was no lower place to go. The fact is, sin will rob you of everything it can every time you give it the chance, and this young man had given it every chance possible. What could he do? The Bible tells us that with a severe famine sweeping the land, "no man gave unto him." He was utterly destitute, with no hope of anything ahead but a slow, miserable death from starvation... well, not quite no hope.

Like an injured limb tingling with restored life and feeling as damaged nerves begin to respond to the brain's instructions once again, his mind began to produce clear, unmuddled thinking for the first time since he left home. Freed at long last from a sin-induced temporary insanity, the Bible says, "he came to himself." Through all the hunger and the misery and the helplessness came this one inspiring, hope-filled realization: "How many hired servants of my father's have bread enough and to spare, and I perish with hunger!

"I will arise and go to my father, and will say unto him, Father, I have sinned against heaven, and before thee,

"And am no more worthy to be called thy son: make me as one of thy hired servants." (Lu. 15:17-19).

Every vestige of the arrogant pride that once filled his heart had disappeared. All he wanted to do was to get back to his father, on whatever terms Dad chose to take him back. He deserved nothing and he knew it, he just hoped beyond hope that his father would let him come home, even if it meant living and working as a common servant. What thrills me is that his decision was not to go home to his town or to his friends or even to the possibility of getting away from the pigs and the famine, He was going home for one reason: "I will arise and go *TO MY FATHER!*" Mom, Dad, I don't care how much money you make, or how beautiful your house is or how comfortable a lifestyle you can afford to provide your family, the

111

most valuable thing in your home is you, and when your loved one "comes to himself" (or herself) in the far country, none of that other stuff means anything—it's *YOU* they'll miss and it's *YOU* they'll be coming home to!

## *The Father Still Waits*

Let's get back to the father, still waiting for his son. Can you imagine the scene at the family estate. Every day Dad makes his way down to the end of the road and continues his search of the distant horizon, praying with all his heart that today will be the day his boy comes home. I can hear one of the new hired hands asking his supervisor, "What does the master do up there every day? And why is he so particular about keeping the calf so well-fed?"

"Oh, it's so sad. He has two sons, you know, but you've only met one of them. The youngest left home and the old man has never been the same since. He keeps the calf fed in case the boy comes home. Every day he goes to the end of the road and just waits, hoping his son will come back someday."

I can see the two of them shaking their heads, pitying their master and glad they did not have such grief to bear. But they really weren't fully grasping what was going on in the heart of the father. Yes, he felt the loss of his son, but his daily vigil wasn't an act of helpless grief, it was done out of love, out of undying hope, out of a determination that no matter what happened, no matter what his son might have done, this father would never give up on him. He wasn't just waiting, he was "sending." In his heart, he was speaking across the miles to his boy, "Come on home, Son. Don't let the mess you're in stop you from coming back to me." It was faith... selfless, unblinking faith like a lighthouse beacon calling out to his wayward son, "Come Home!"

As Dad took up his position that day, once more his ageing eyes began to squint and focus on a barely visible dip on the far horizon. "When he comes, he'll have to come that way," thought Dad. And, as he must have done countless times before, he began to pray and ask God to keep his boy safe and bring him home soon. A figure appears. Growing larger as he slowly comes a little closer, Dad's heart begins to race. But the figure turns and starts moving off in a different direction, and Dad heaves a sigh. "It's only my neighbor's servant checking the herds. He does it every day about this time." Two or three more times that day, another little movement would appear on the edge of Dad's ever-straining vision, briefly setting his emotions on fire, only to extinguish that fire as whoever it was continued on their particular journey. Despite the emotional roller coaster he must have put himself through every day, his diligence never wavered, his distant gaze never faltered.

### Home At Last!

Once more a faraway little dot comes into view. "Whoever it is isn't moving very quickly," thought

Dad. The endless minutes pass, and Dad steels himself for yet another let-down, but all his hopes and dreams rush to the surface again in spite of himself. "He hasn't turned away yet. Wait, what's he doing? Has he stopped?"

The boy can hardly put one foot in front of the other, he's so weak from hunger. Pausing for breath, he somehow finds the strength to lift his head, and that's when he finally sees the familiar shape of home in the distance. "I think that's it. Yes, I'd know father's house anywhere. I can't believe I'm almost there." Tears fill his eyes, and he doesn't notice the lone figure waiting at the end of the road.

But Dad is noticing him. As the boy inches closer, Dad's eyes are opening wider by the second. "Is it... no... it can't be... wait... he... he's too thin to me my boy, but... Oh, yes, yes. It is him! It is him!" At the top of his voice he starts screaming out in uncontrollable joy. "It's him! It's him! My boy's come home... Oh, thank you, Lord, my boy's come home!"

Taking off at a speed the elders of the city would have deemed far too undignified for a man of his station, Dad ran with all his might towards the frail, struggling figure in the distance. Arms raised, voice lifted high in praise to God, leaping and howling for joy as he went, there wasn't a younger man within miles who could have out paced him.

The boy, head bowed low as he walked, all but ready to collapse with exhaustion, didn't see him at first. But I know before Dad was two hundred yards away, he heard him. "Who in the world? Dad? That can't be..." Mustering the strength from somewhere, I can imagine him calling out, "Dad, is that really you?" Before he had time to call the second time, Dad ran into him so hard he almost knocked the wind right out of him. The Bible describes the scene with unmatchable eloquence:

"But when he was yet a great way off, his father saw him, and had compassion, and ran, and fell on his neck, and kissed him." (Lu. 15:20).

He had prepared a speech for his father, but before he could even finish it, long before he got to the part about being taken back as a hired servant, the father took control of the situation.

"But the father said to his servants, Bring forth the best robe, and put it on him; and put a ring on his hand, and shoes on his feet:

"And bring hither the fatted calf, and kill it; and let us eat, and be merry:

"For this my son was dead, and is alive again; he was lost, and is found. And they began to be merry." (Lu. 15:22-24).

No doubt about it, this boy was home! The object of a father's undying, unrelenting love, he was given the best robe, fed with the best food, and unreservedly welcomed back into his father's house. Instantly restored to him were all the rights and privileges of, not a servant, but a son.

### God's Heart Of Love

I hope you'll forgive me if I've taken a few liberties with the story, but it's not hard for me to imagine the emotions at play in this situation. As I noted earlier, we can all identify with this father's initial sorrow, and we can all clearly relate to how it must have felt to welcome his lost son home again. Jesus told the story this way because no one would have trouble seeing the unfolding drama in their mind's eye. My purpose in relating it to you here is to help remind you of your Heavenly Father's love, not only for you, but for every last one of your family. There isn't a single soul—not one—for whom He doesn't keep scanning the horizon, for whom He doesn't have a robe prepared, for whom He hasn't prepared a magnificent celebration feast. As the old hymn says,

> *If we with ink the ocean filled,*
> *And were the sky of parchment made,*
> *Were every stalk on earth a quill,*
> *And every man a scribe by trade,*
> *To write the love of God above,*
> *Would drain the ocean dry,*
> *Nor could the scroll contain the whole,*
> *Though stretched from sky to sky.*

This wonderful stanza, superlatively eloquent though it is, only begins to explore the immensity of God's love. As you pray for your loved ones, remember that as much as you love them, He loves them more. His love reaches across the miles, over the bitter breaches of family strife, through the emptiness, waste and destruction inflicted on your family members by sin, and whispers deep into their heart that if they'll just come "home," they'll find Him waiting... and you'll be waiting, too! Let me echo the words of the Apostle Paul: "For I am persuaded, that neither death, nor life, nor angels, nor principalities, nor powers, nor things present, nor things to come, Nor height, nor depth, nor any other creature, shall be able to separate us from the love of God, which is in Christ Jesus our Lord." (Ro. 8:38,39).

I love that verse. Just look at the list of all the things that CAN NOT separate us from the love of God. It tells me that if none of these things can separate us from the love of God, NOTHING ELSE CAN! With all my heart, I believe your loved ones don't have to be separated from His love either. I restate my earlier position that everyone has a free will and therefore has the God-given right to determine their own spiritual destiny, but when the awesome love of God is at work on our behalf, what—or who—is able to resist it? I don't have a single doubt anywhere in my being that you have it in your power to impact your unsaved loved one's lives in ways that make it all but inevitable that they will come face to face with the eternal, fathomless love of God. That's something they might try to withstand or even ignore for a while, but, if you're not willing to give up on them, God can even reach them in the pig-pen!

Everything we've said so far comes down to this: When it comes to winning your loved ones to Christ, what you do matters. Follow just a few of the guidelines we've discussed in this book and I believe you can change the entire destiny of your family—and gloriously alter the future for entire generations to come!

# Epilogue

## From The Promise To The Palace

There are two men in Scripture who were made rather astonishing promises by God. One, whose life we looked at, is Joseph; the other is David. When Joseph was a very young man, God made him a promise that his entire family would bow down before him. That simply didn't make any sense given the traditions of the day and the circumstances in which he found himself. It took a very long time for that unlikely promise to become a reality, and during that time, Joseph endured enormous hardships. He was thrown into a pit, sold into slavery, thrown into prison, and given up for dead. But one day, God elevated faithful Joseph to the highest office in Egypt, second only to Pharaoh himself. He was finally in the esteemed position he had been promised, but there was a lot that happened between the promise and the palace.

David was nothing more than a shepherd boy, the youngest of eight sons. Even his own father considered him so insignificant that when Samuel the prophet came to see the family, David was left

119

outside to look after the sheep. But God rejected David's older brothers, and that day, Samuel anointed David to be the King of Israel. There was just one problem—Saul was still on the throne!

On the day Samuel anointed him, David was not much more than a boy. Years would pass before Saul died and David took the throne of Judah. Seven more years of bloody war would pass before he became, finally, king of all Israel at the age of thirty-seven. Between the promise and the palace were years of brutal hardship, danger, continual struggle, even one point when he almost lost his entire family after the Amalekites raided the city of Ziklag (1 Sam. 30). Once again, a lot happened between the promise and the palace.

You, like Joseph and David, have been made an incredible promise by God Himself: "Believe on the Lord Jesus Christ, and thou shalt be saved, *AND THY HOUSE.*" (Ac. 16:31). But, just like for those two great men, there may be much for you to face between today and the day you see that promise become a reality. It may not be an actual palace you're after, but what you do want is your unsaved loved ones to join you in service to Christ, where He is the Head and the King over your entire household, and your family worship Him as one, united as His loyal subjects. What stands between your promise and your "palace" I can't tell you, I only know that to decide to lay hold of the promise is to decide to do battle in the spiritual realm. However, as we said back in the beginning, this is a battle we can win, and